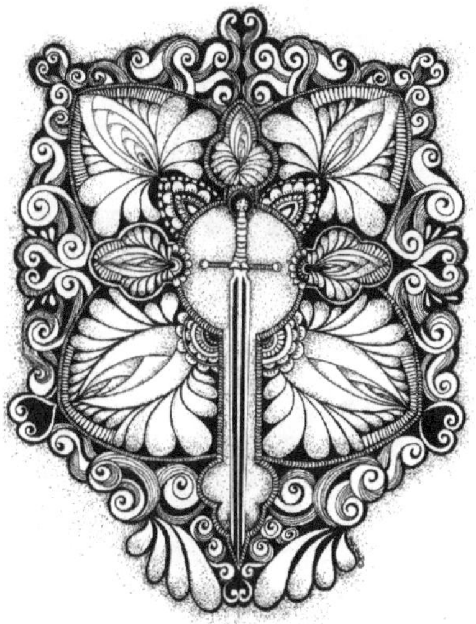

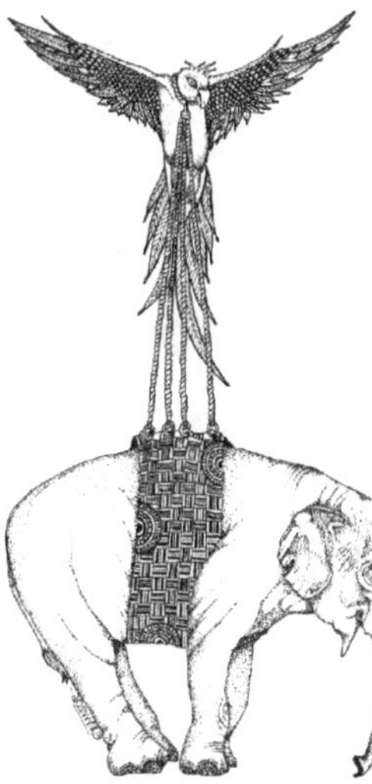

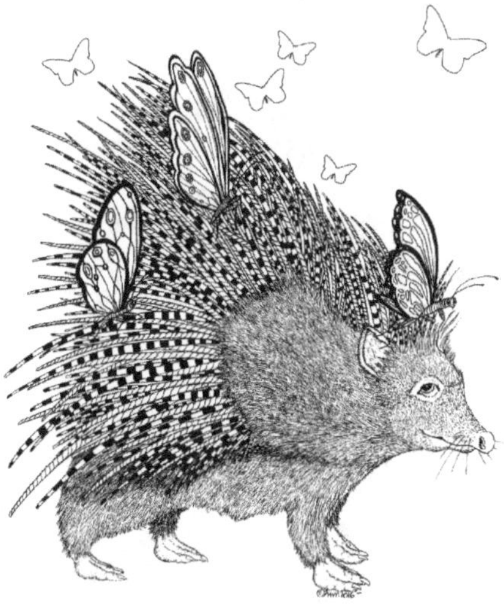

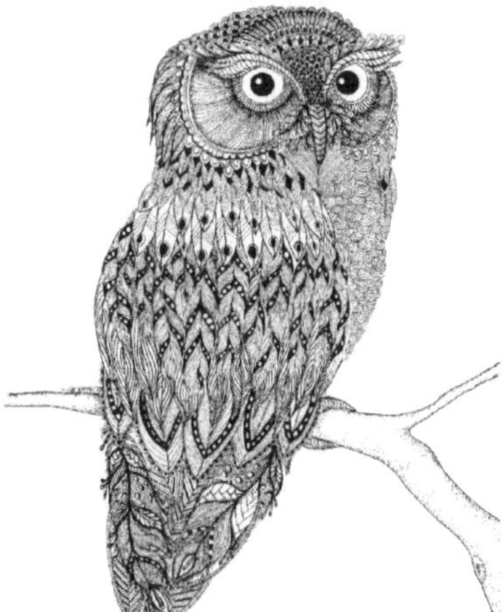

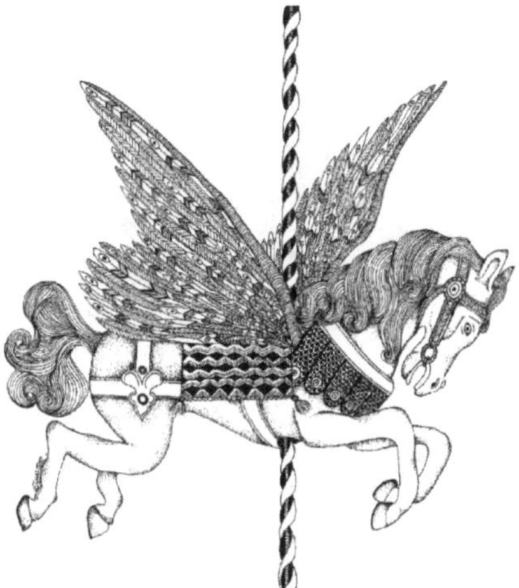

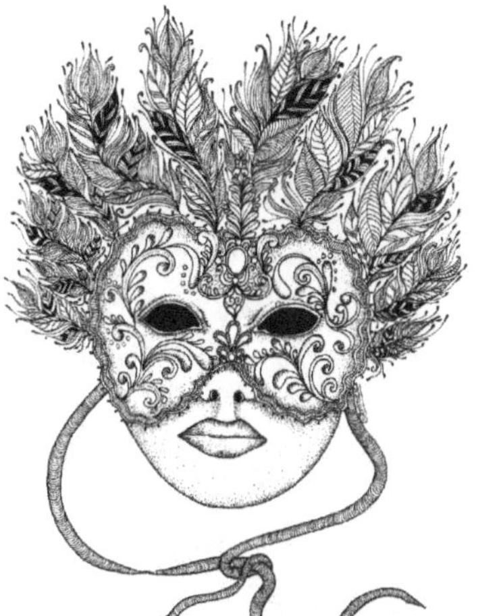

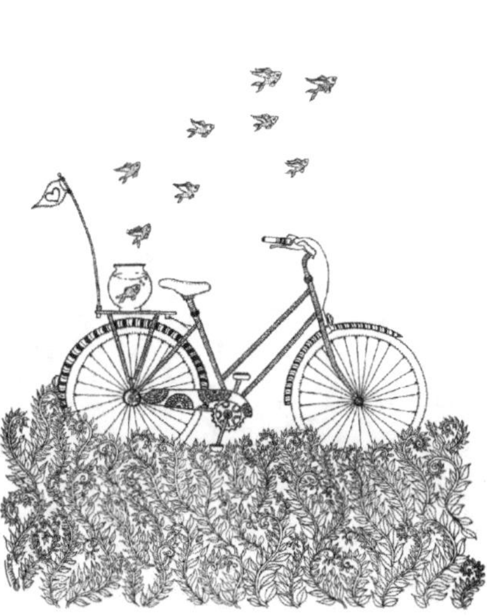

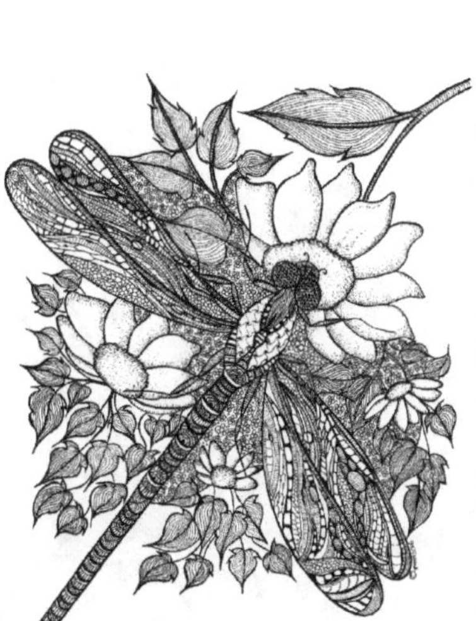

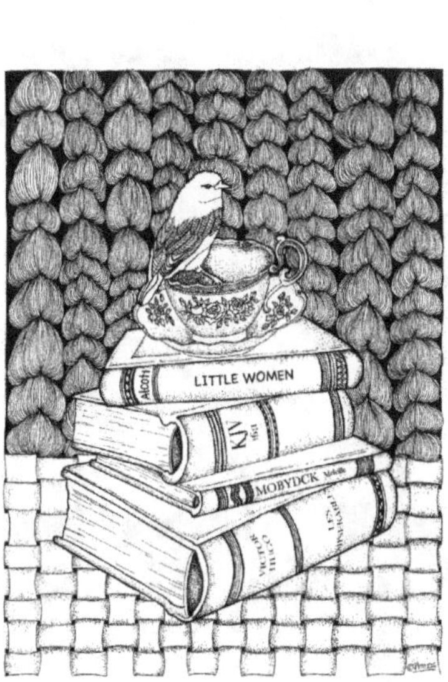

Adult Coloring Book

A COLORING FEAST

35 Relaxing Illustrations to Color

www.ivetteramoslevy.com

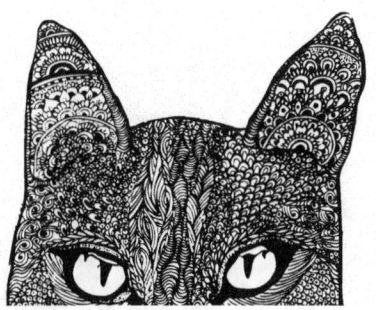

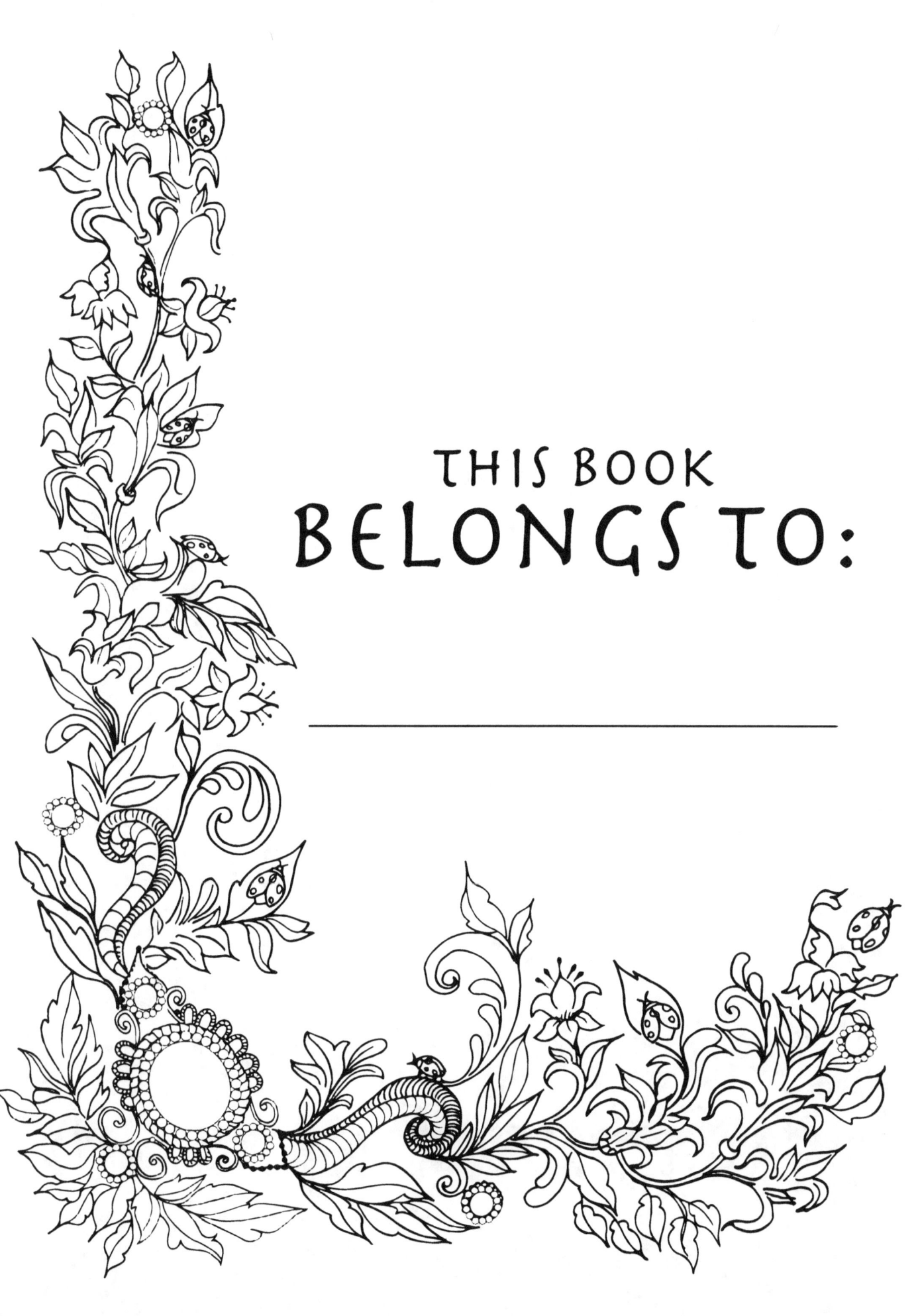

THIS BOOK
BELONGS TO:

_____

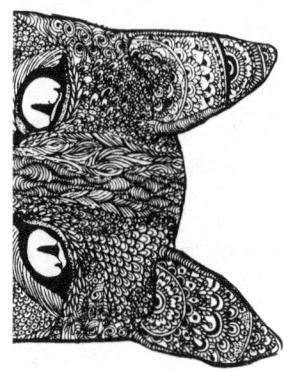

Ivette Ramos Levy is a
fine artist, illustrator
and muralist.
She studied graphic design,
stained glass and glass fusing
in Mexico; techniques in clay,
glass fusing and painting in
Italy; and glass fusing in the U.S.
She has illustrated five books,
both in the United States and
in Mexico. She lives in North
Texas with her family.

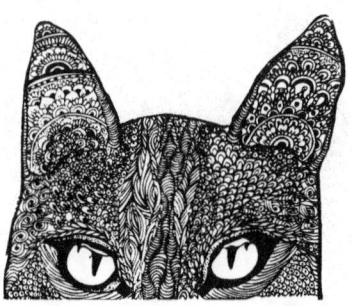

INTRODUCTION

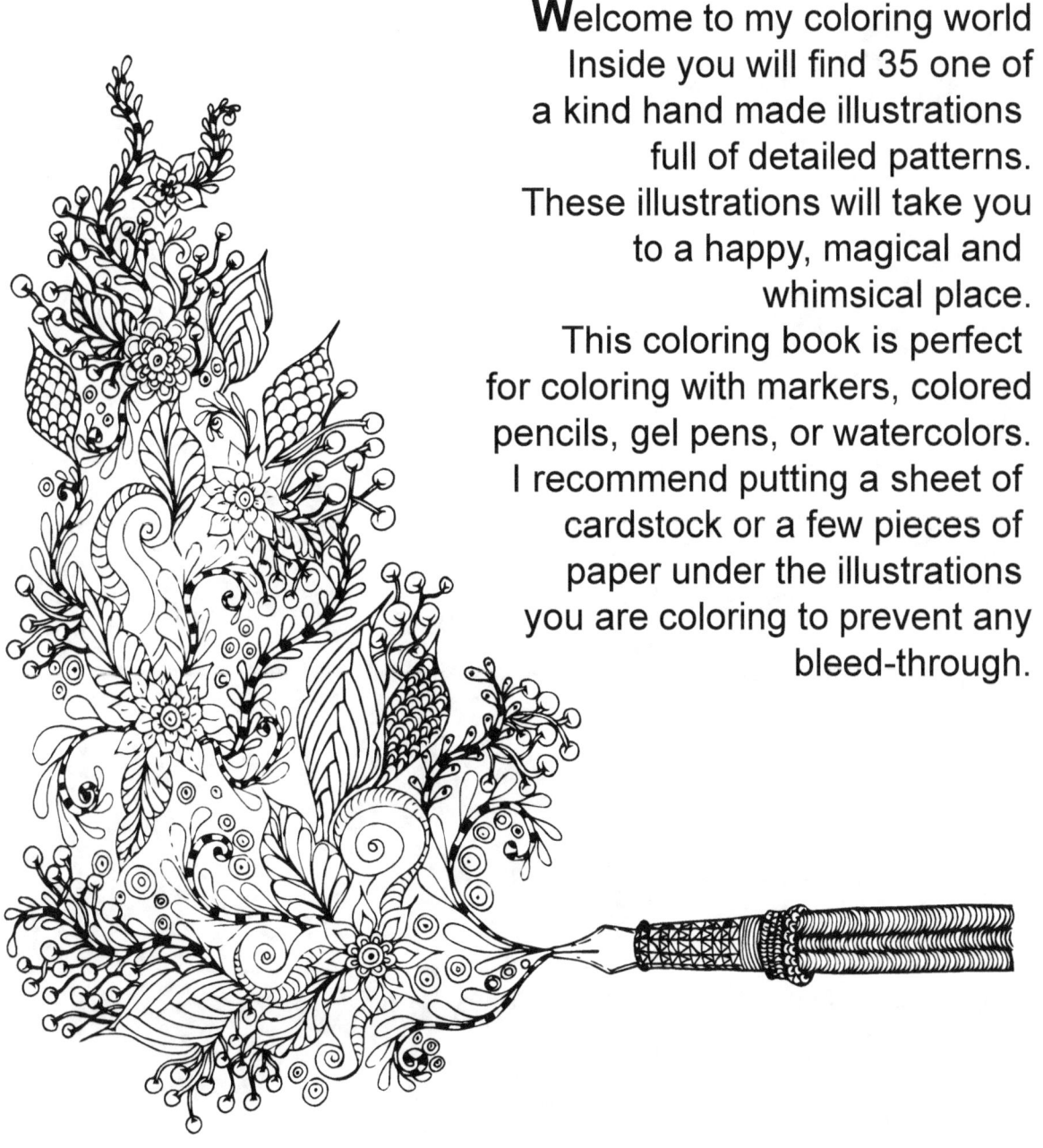

Welcome to my coloring world
Inside you will find 35 one of
a kind hand made illustrations
full of detailed patterns.
These illustrations will take you
to a happy, magical and
whimsical place.
This coloring book is perfect
for coloring with markers, colored
pencils, gel pens, or watercolors.
I recommend putting a sheet of
cardstock or a few pieces of
paper under the illustrations
you are coloring to prevent any
bleed-through.

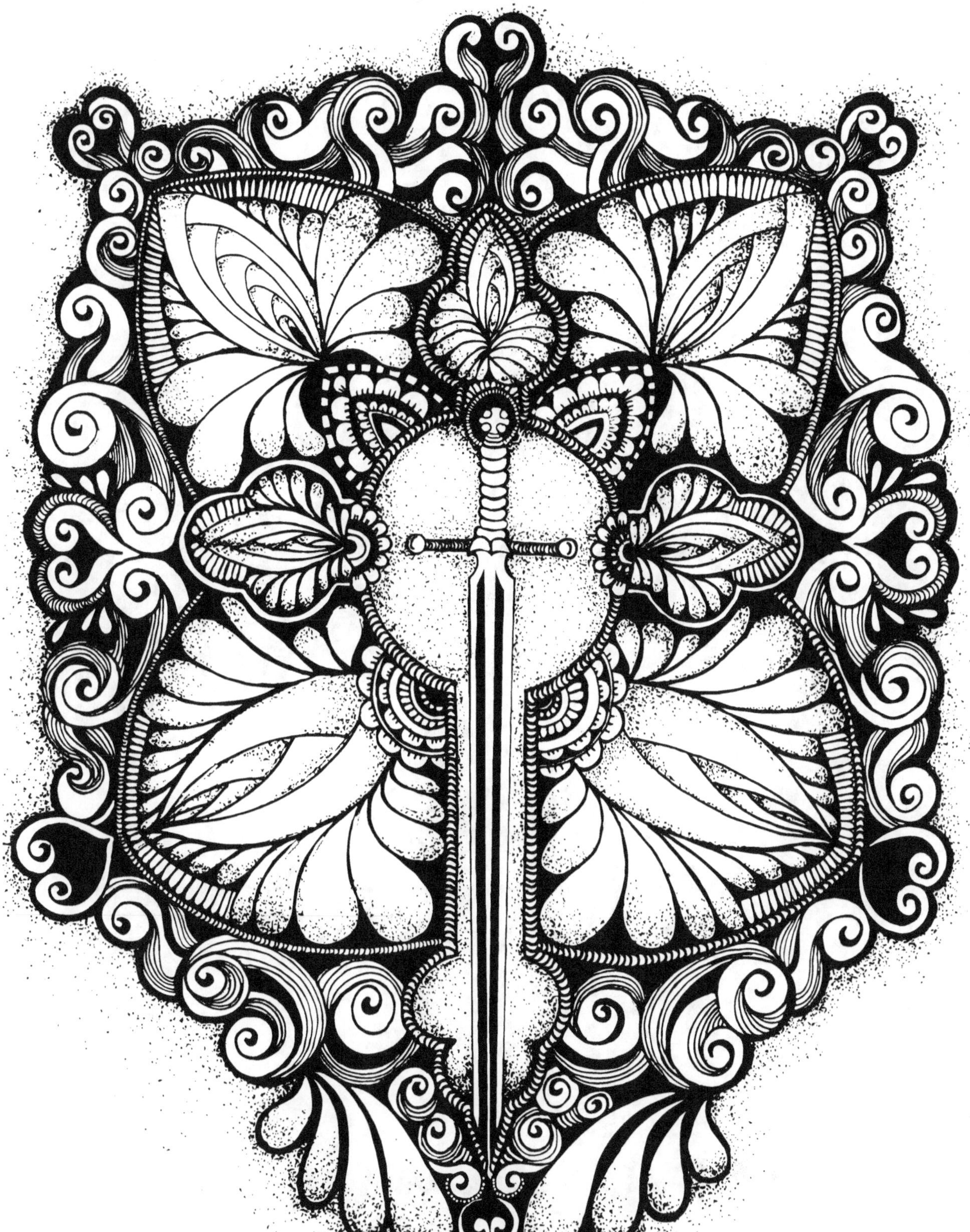

Artist:©IvetteRamosLevy Colorist:___________

Artist:©IvetteRamosLevy Colorist:________________

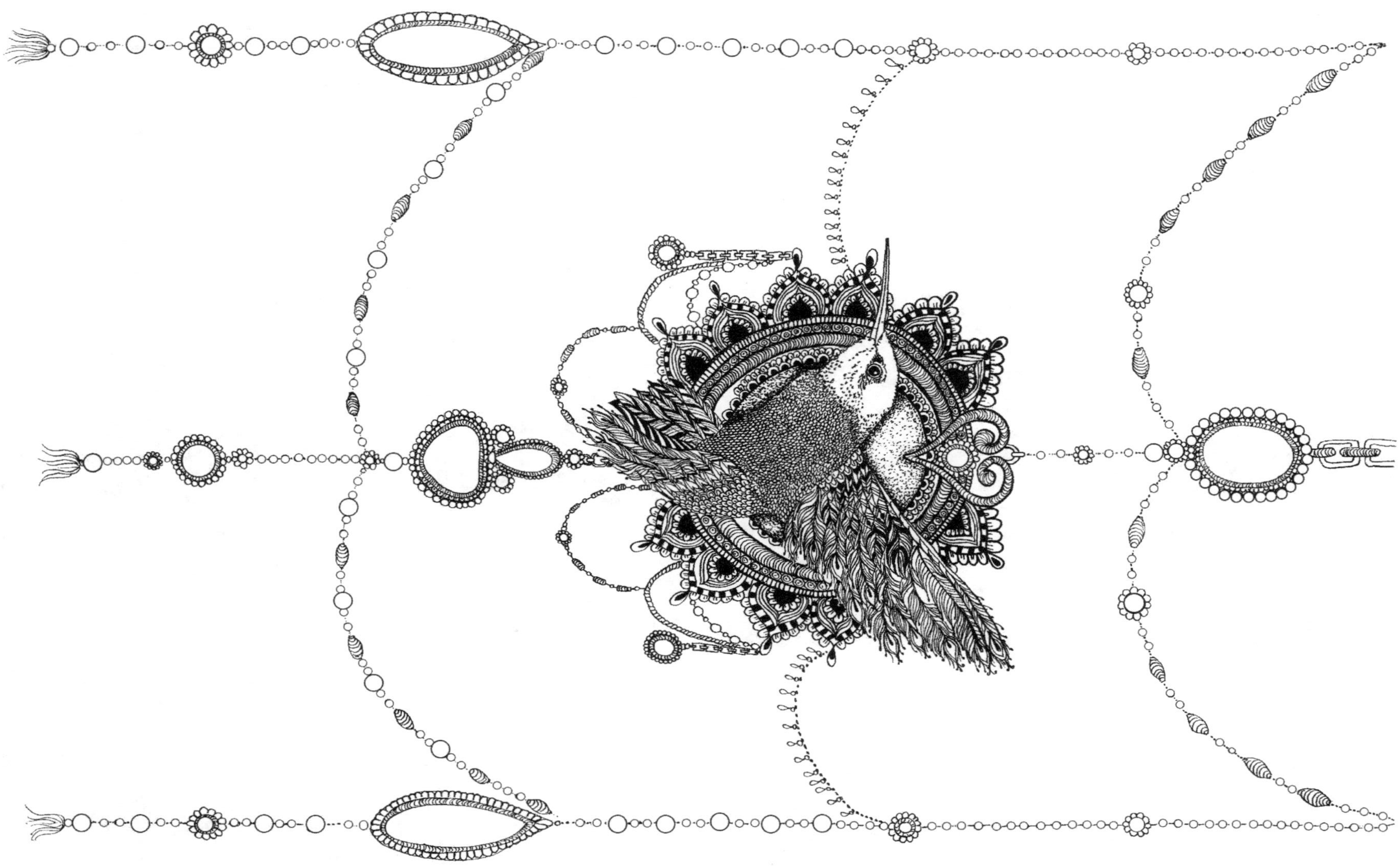

LITTLE WOMEN

Alcott

KJV 1611

MOBYDCK Melville

VICTOR HUGO

LES MISERABLE

Artist:©IvetteRamosLevy Colorist:___________

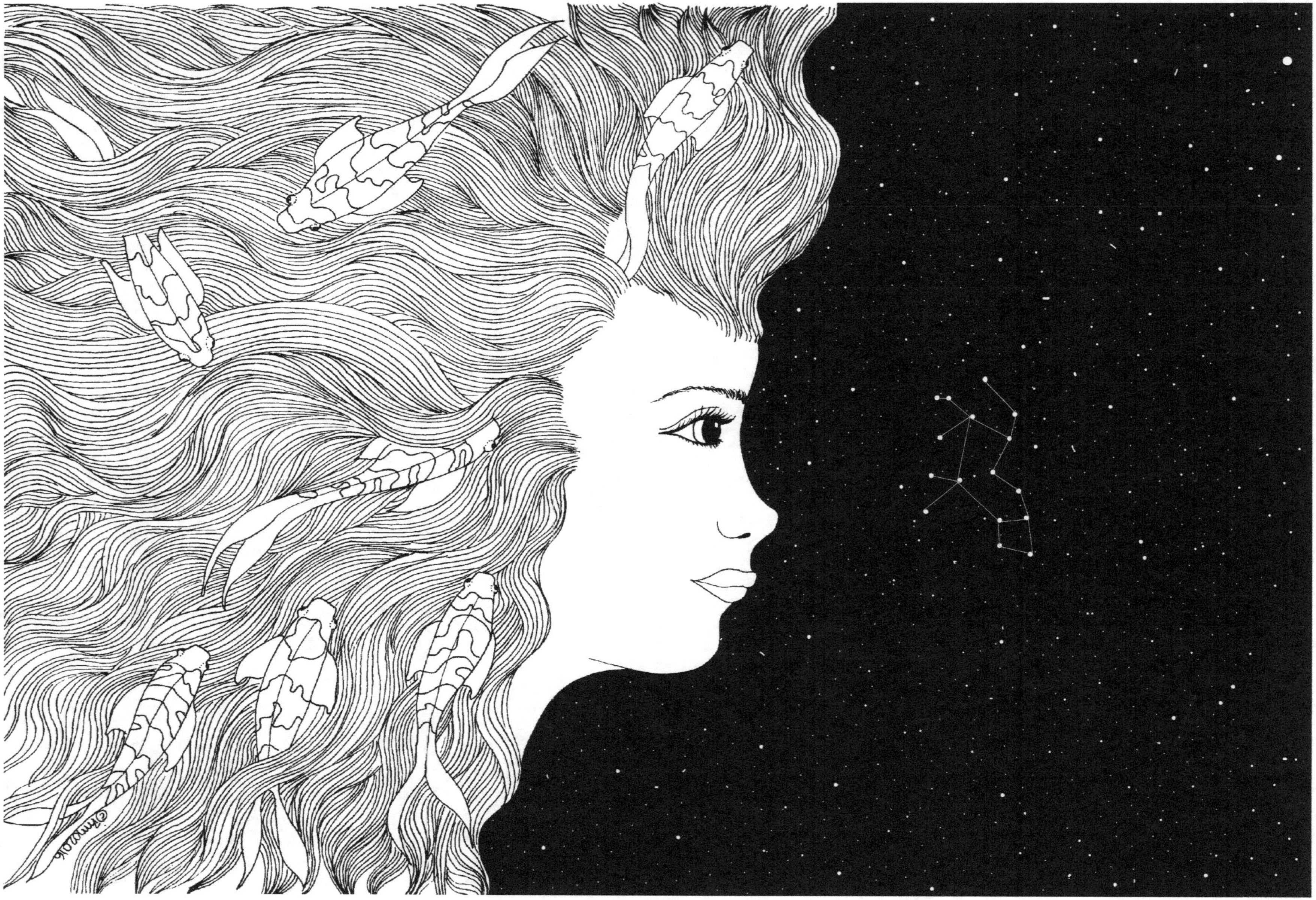

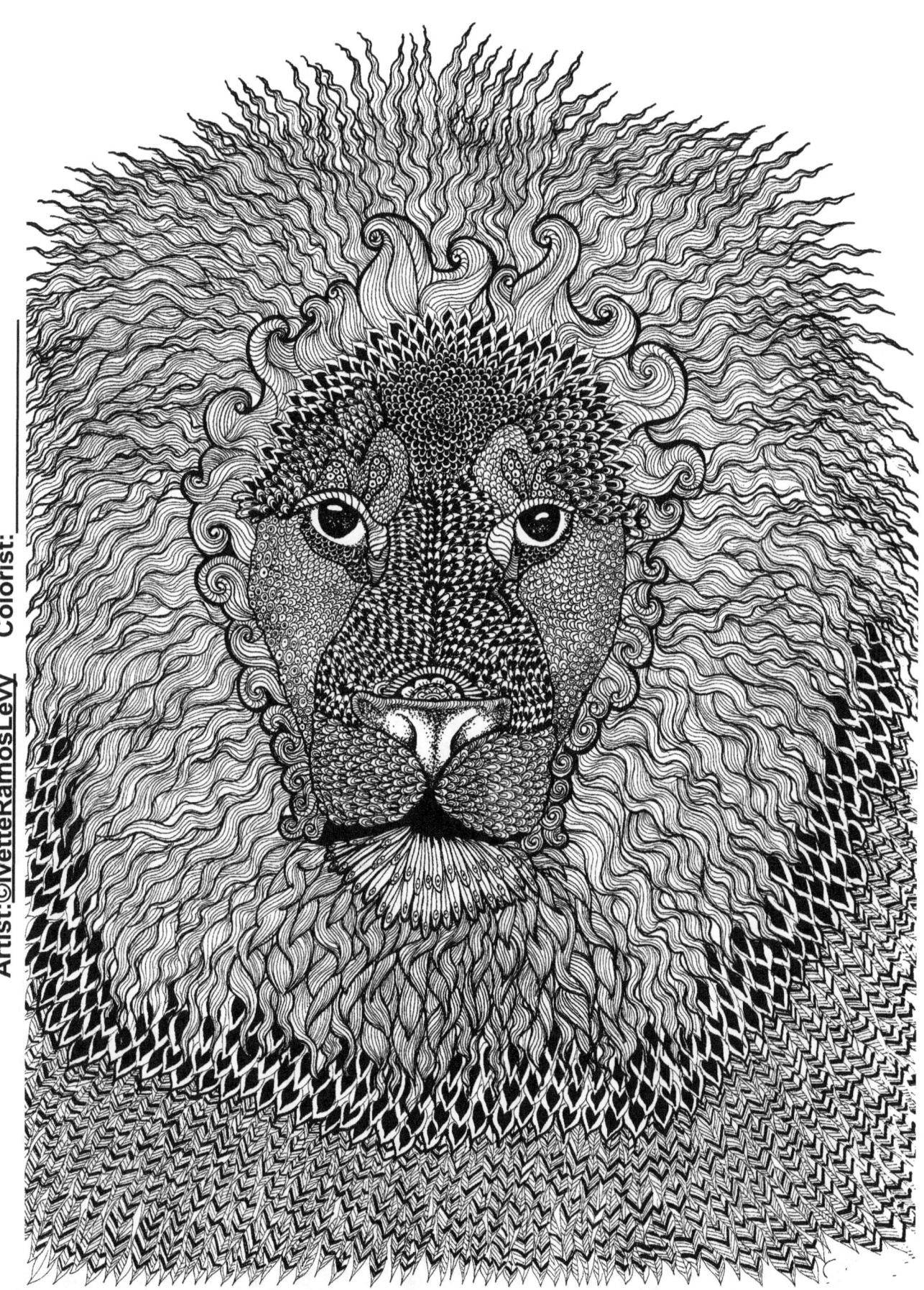

Artist:©IvetteRamosLevy Colorist:____________

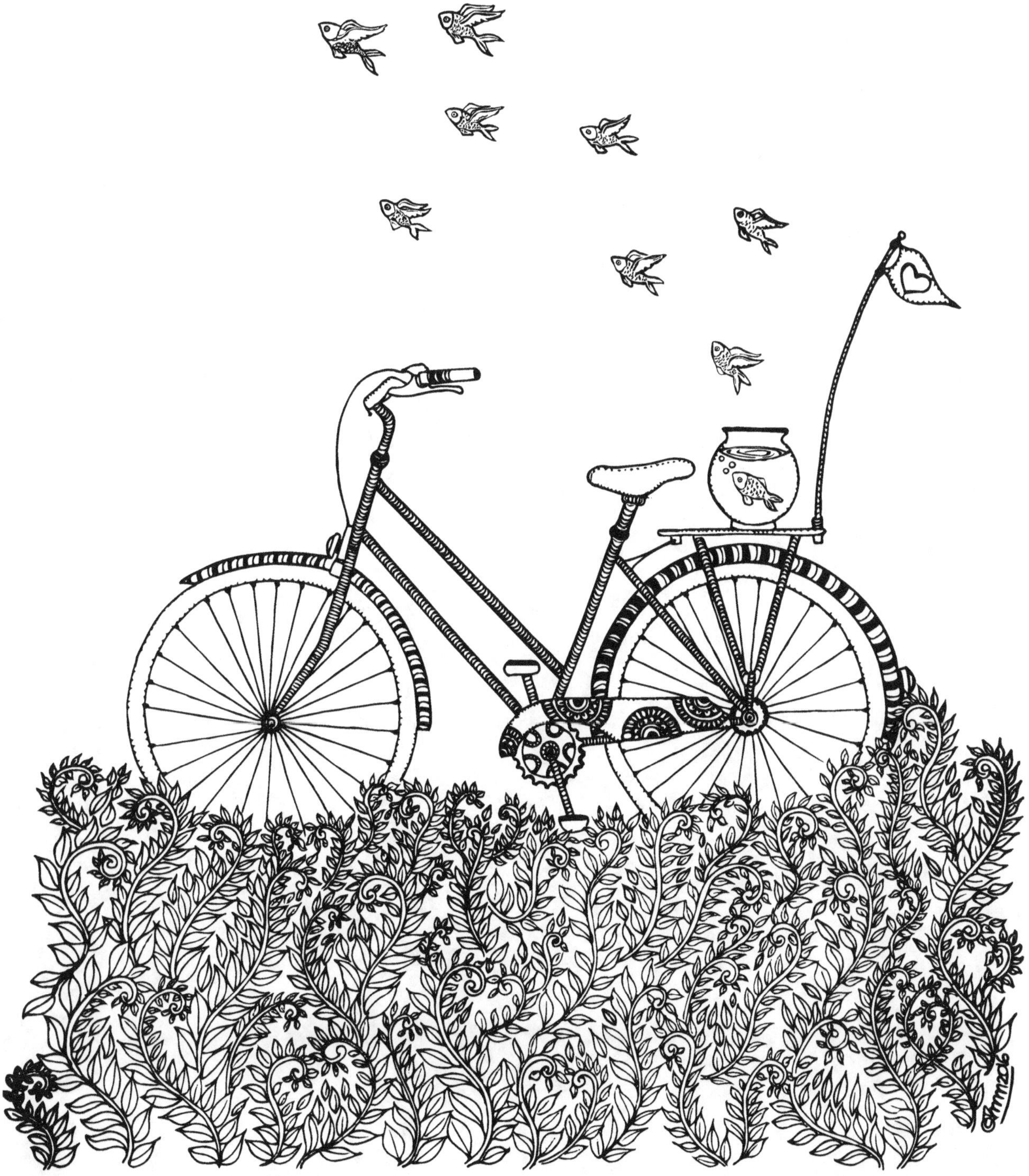

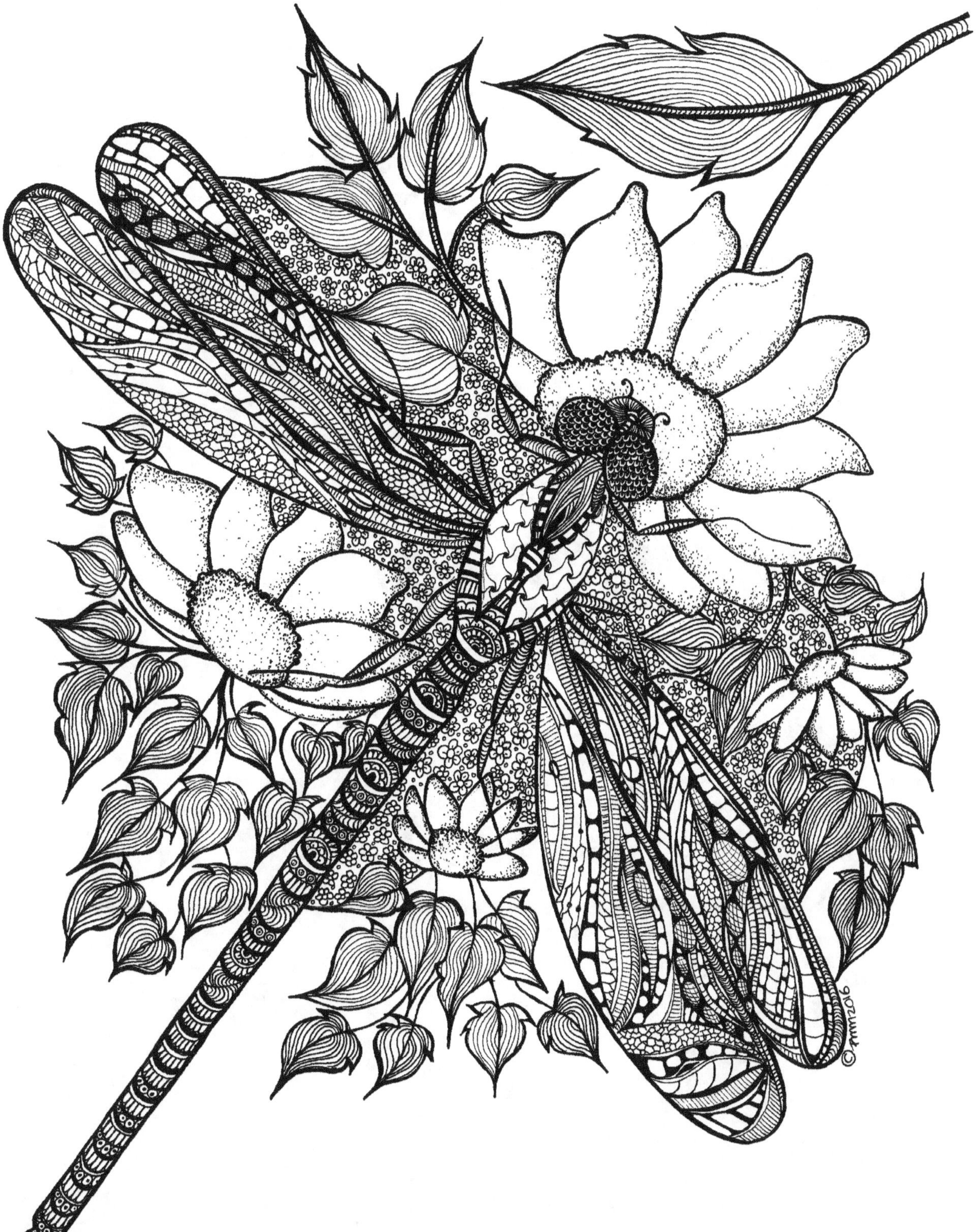

Artist:©IvetteRamosLevy Colorist:____________

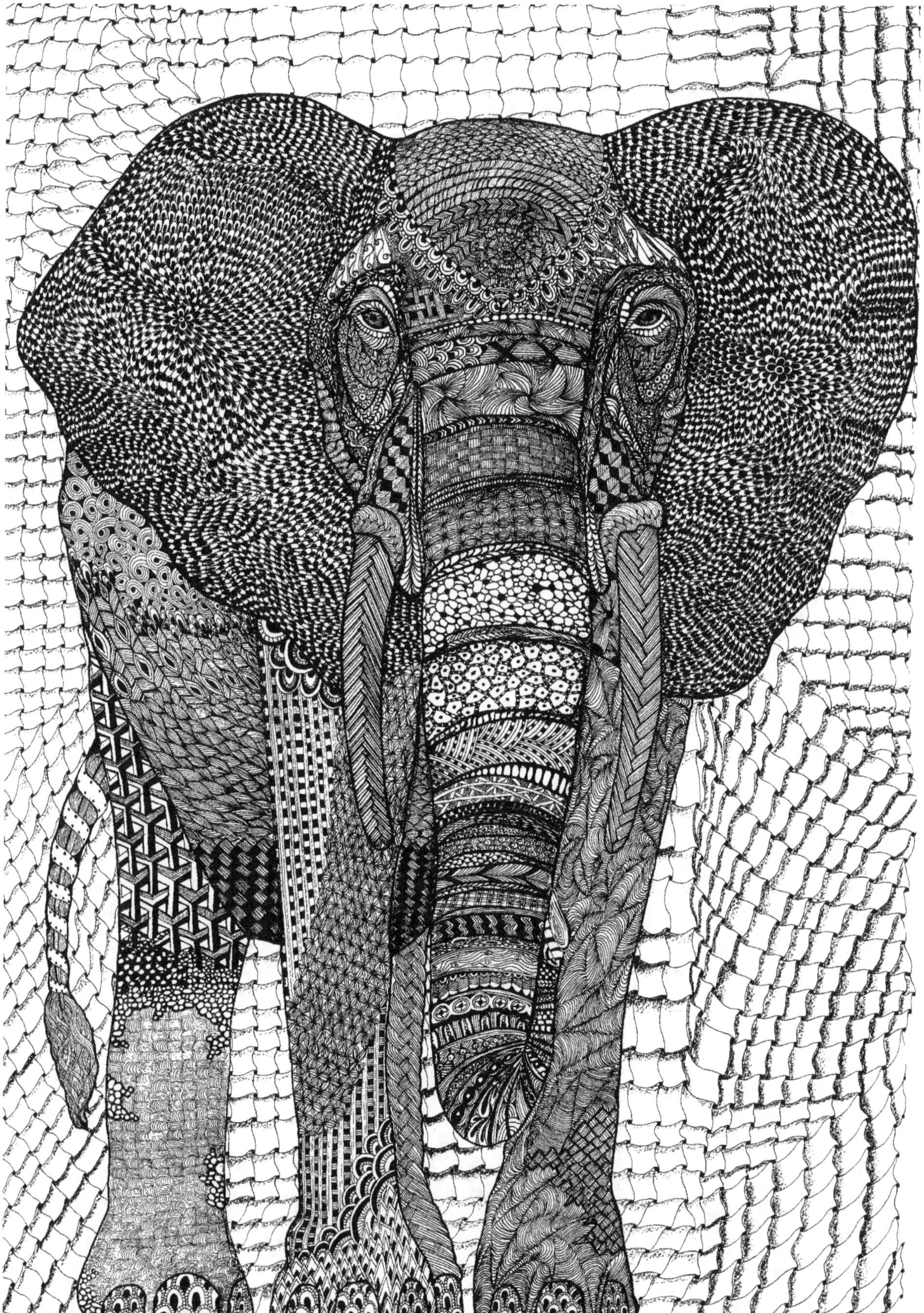

Artist:©IvetteRamosLevy Colorist: ____________

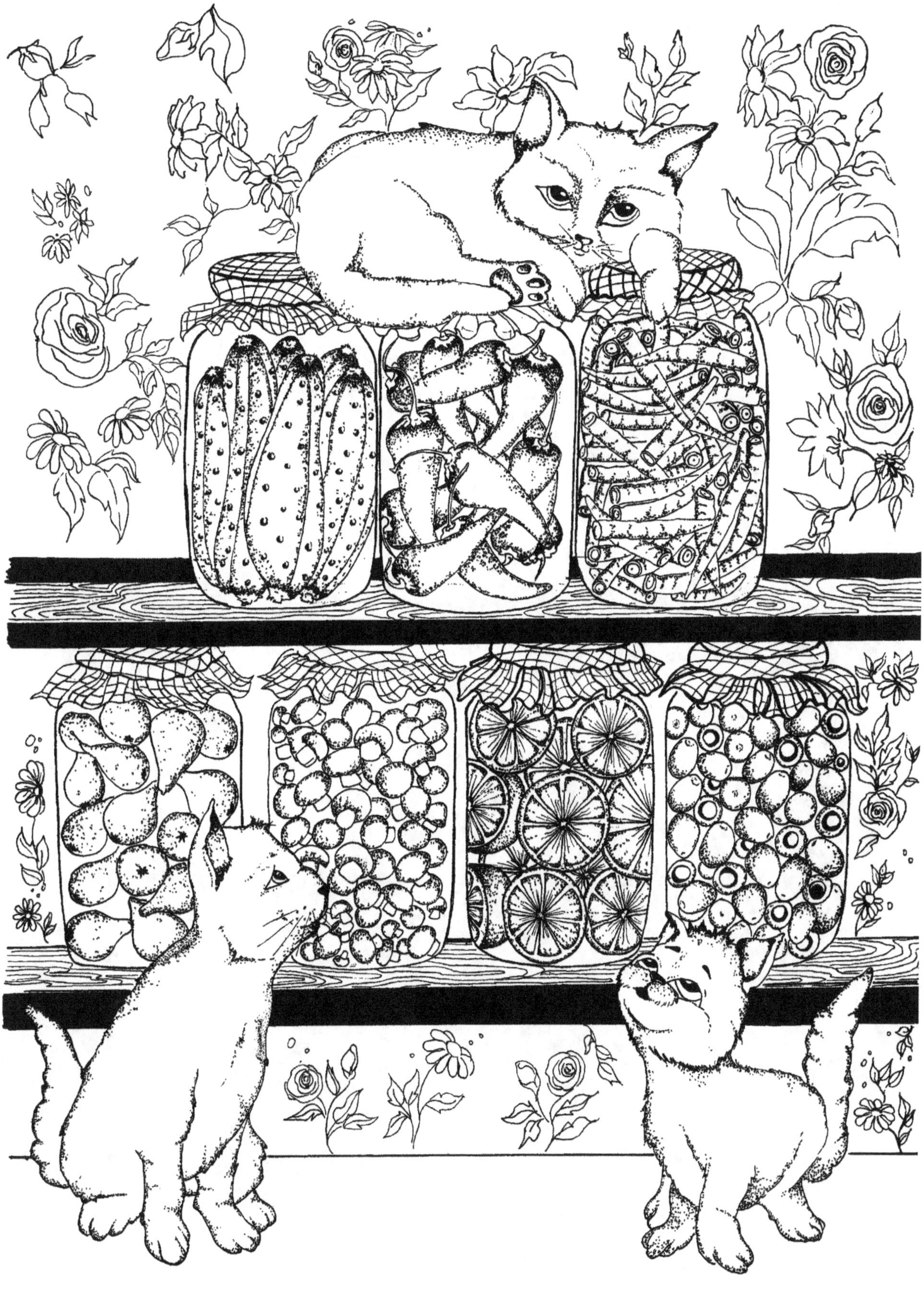

Artist:©IvetteRamosLevy Colorist:

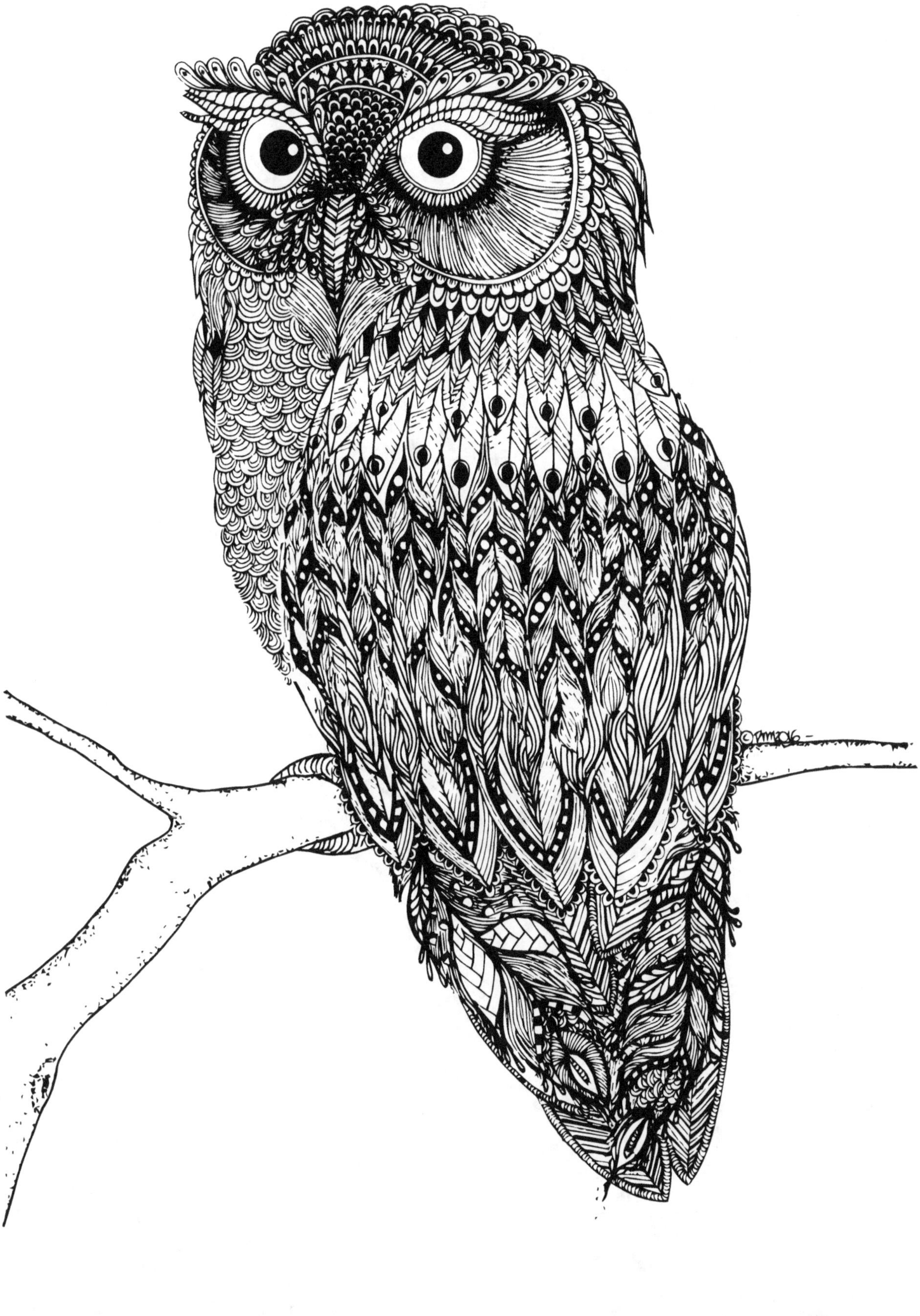

Artist:©IvetteRamosLevy Colorist:____________

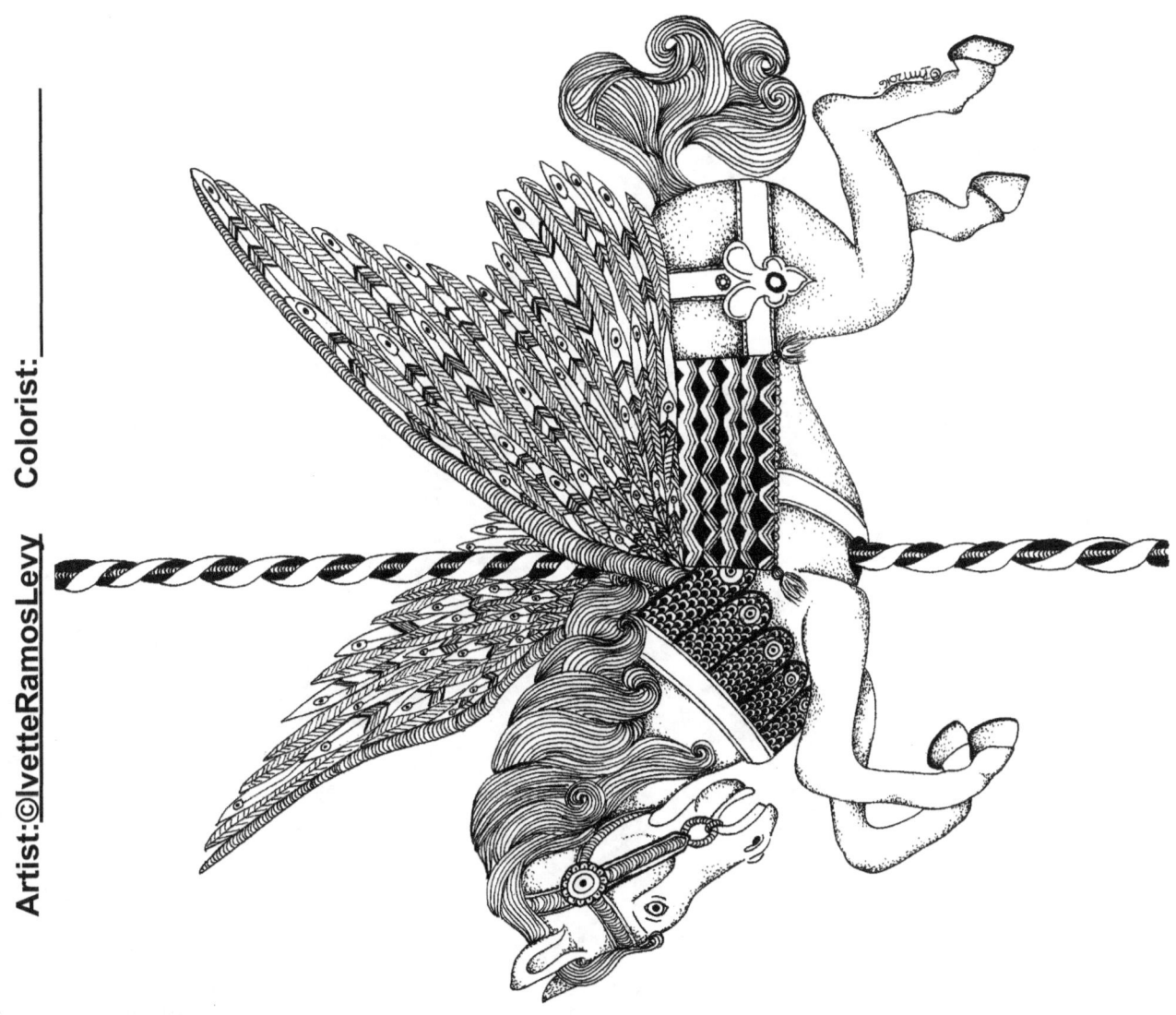

Artist:©IvetteRamosLevy Colorist:____________

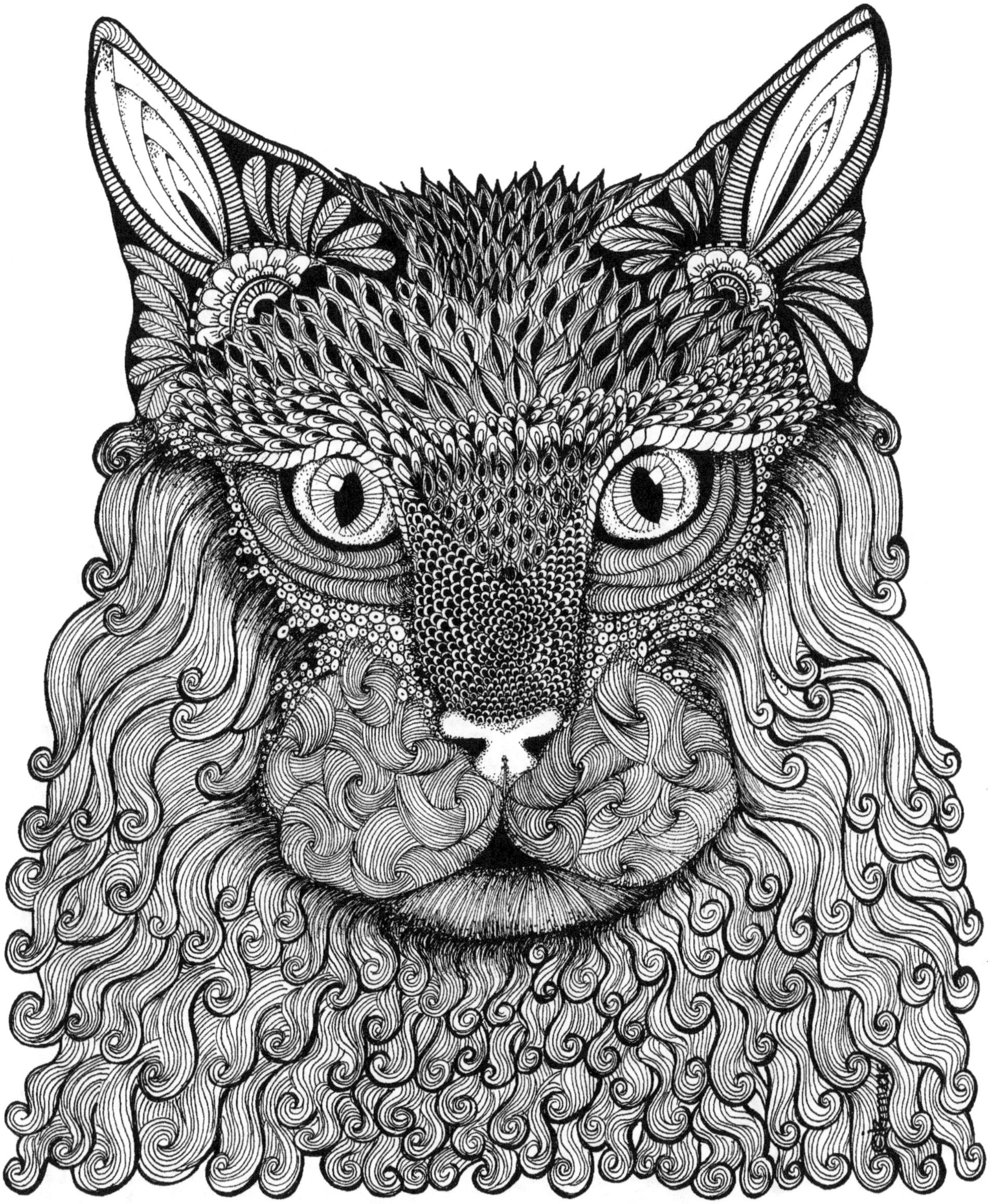

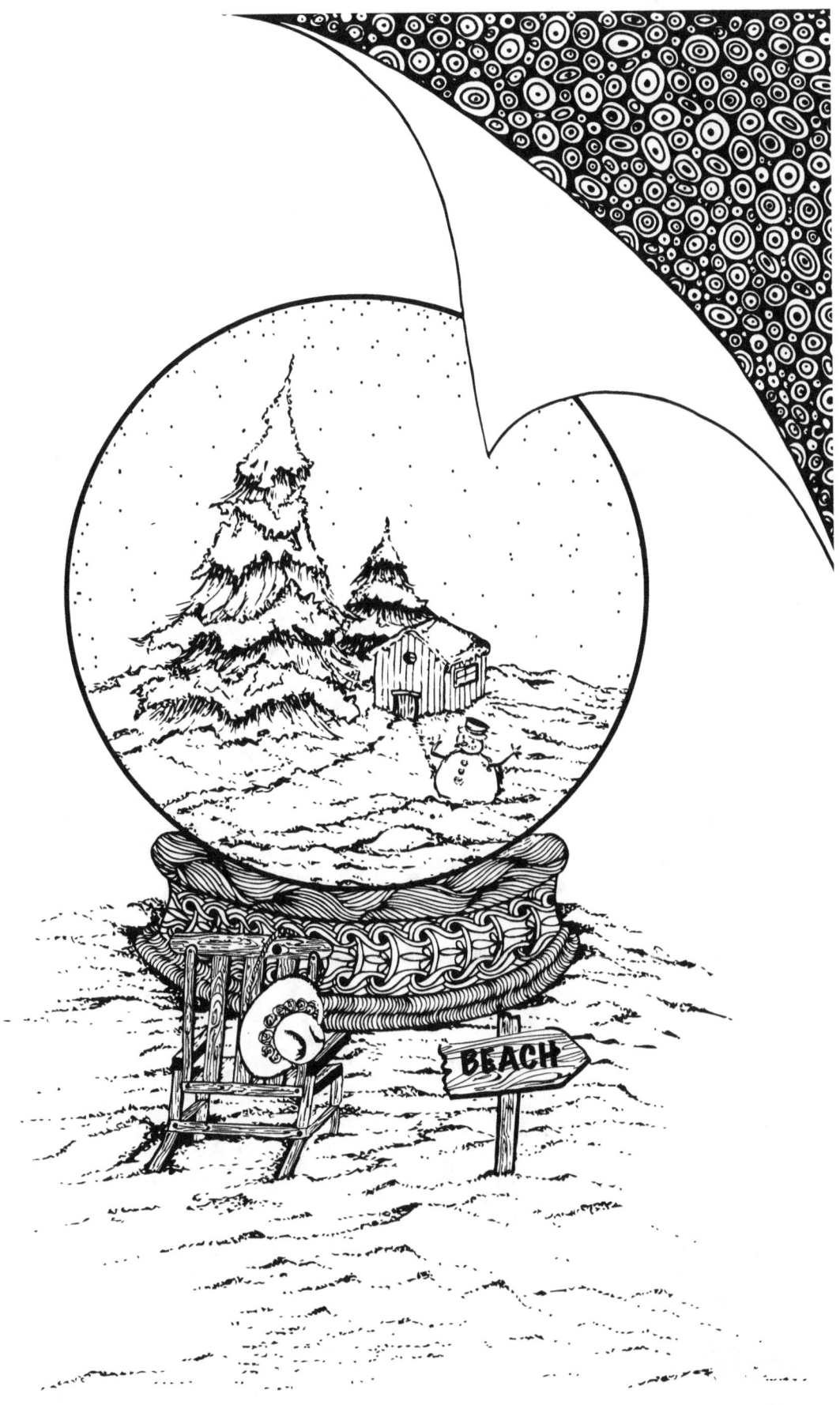

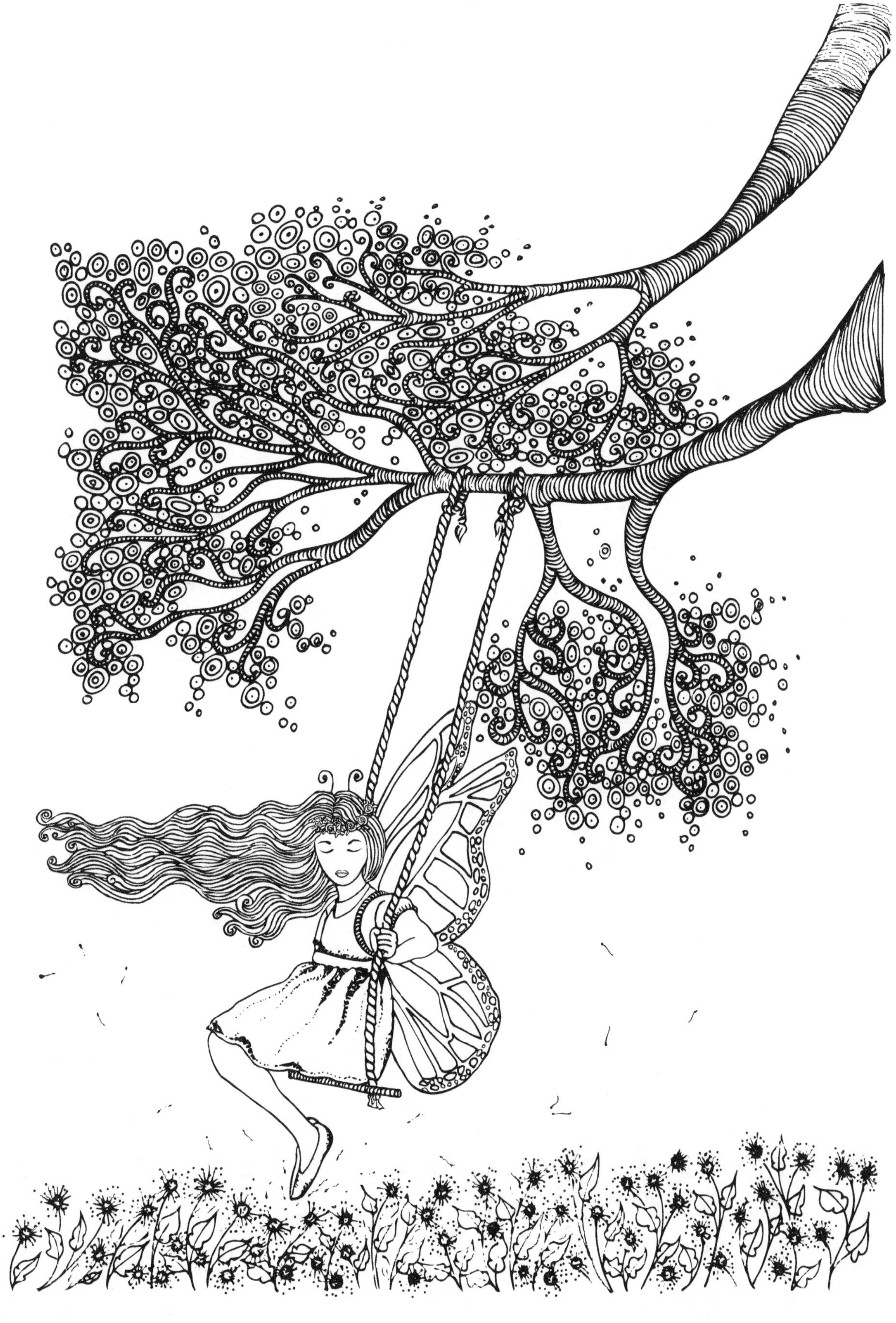

Artist:©IvetteRamosLevy Colorist:____________

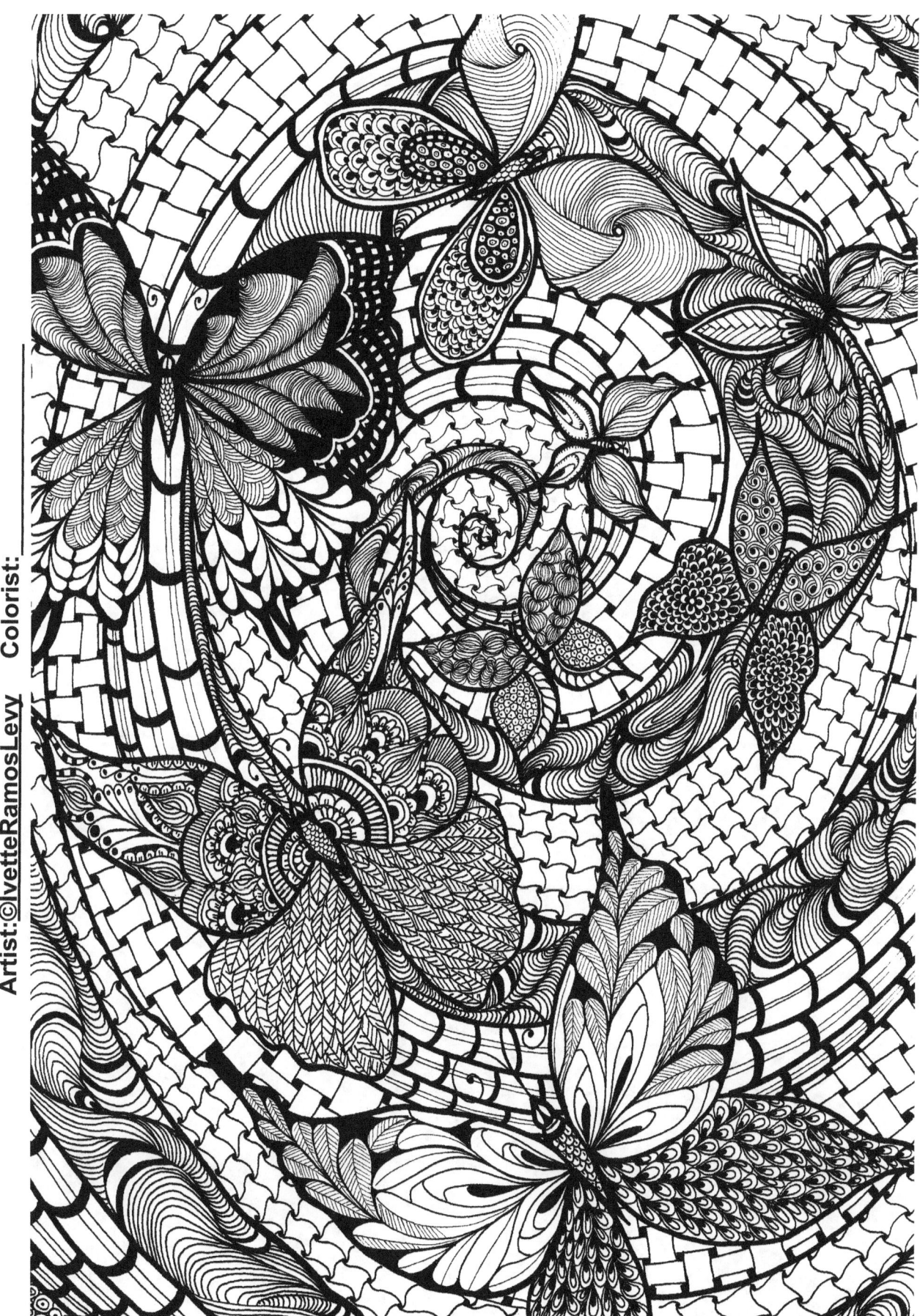

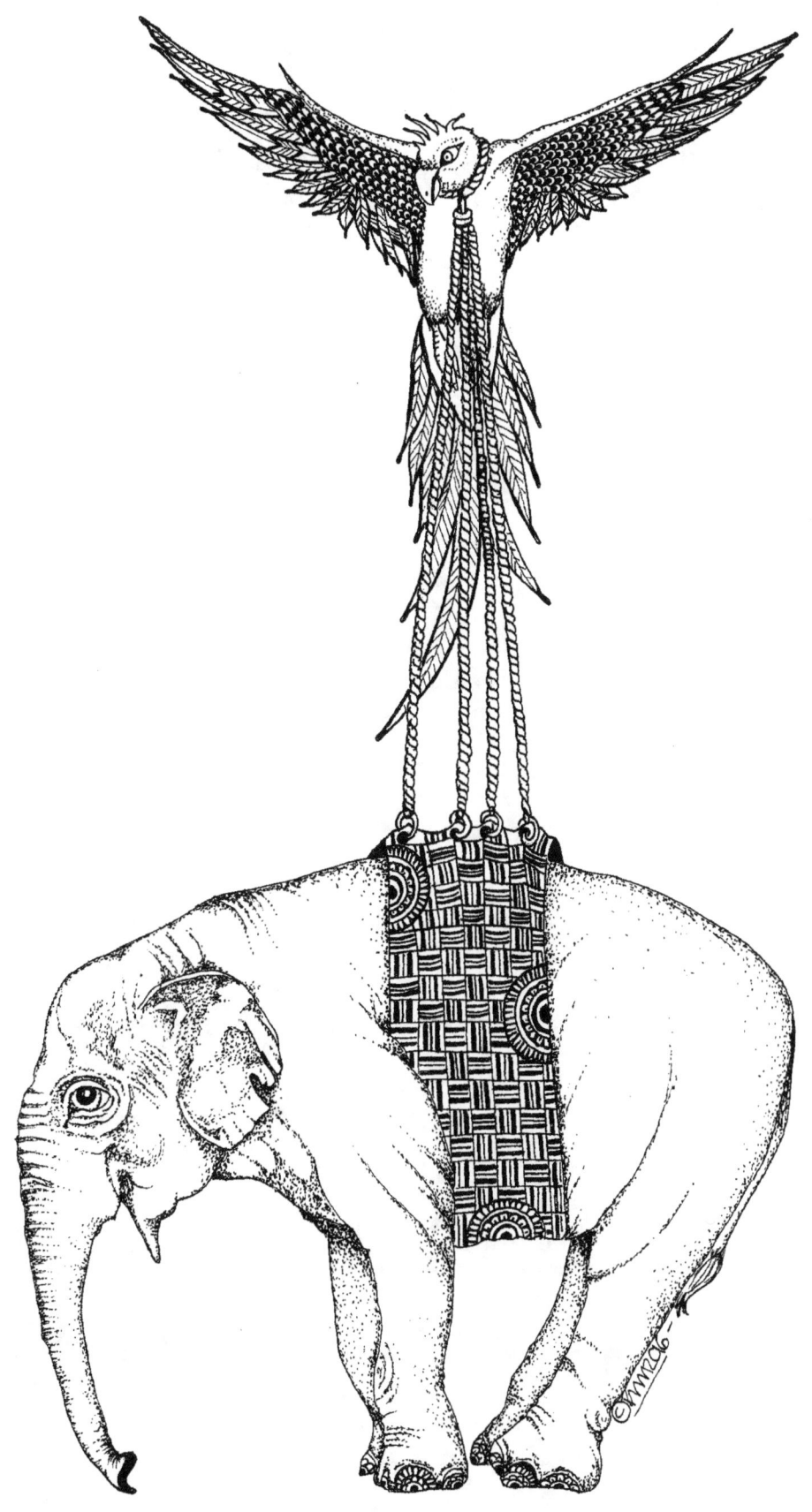

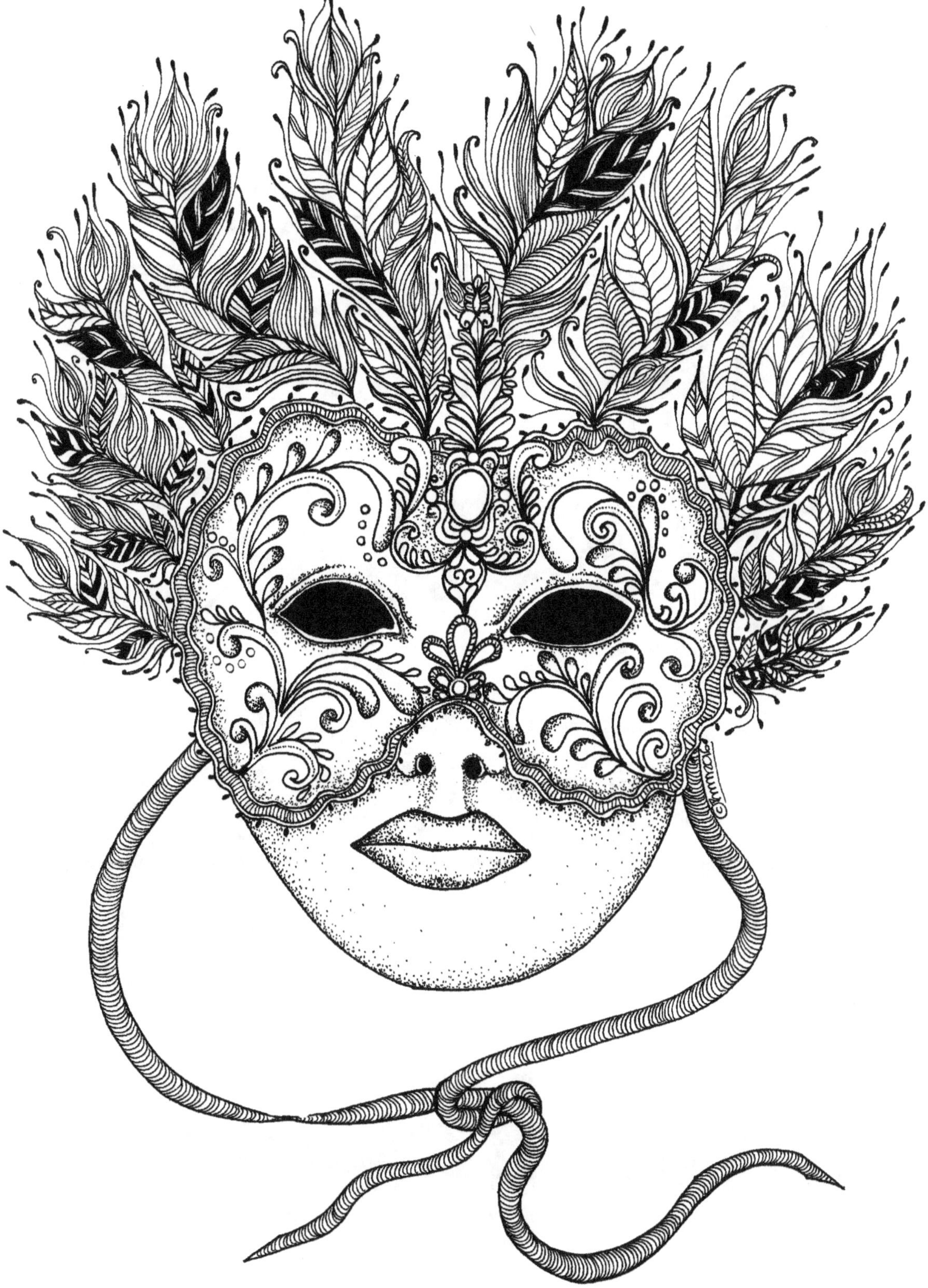

Artist:©IvetteRamosLevy Colorist:________

Artist:©IvetteRamosLevy Colorist:___________

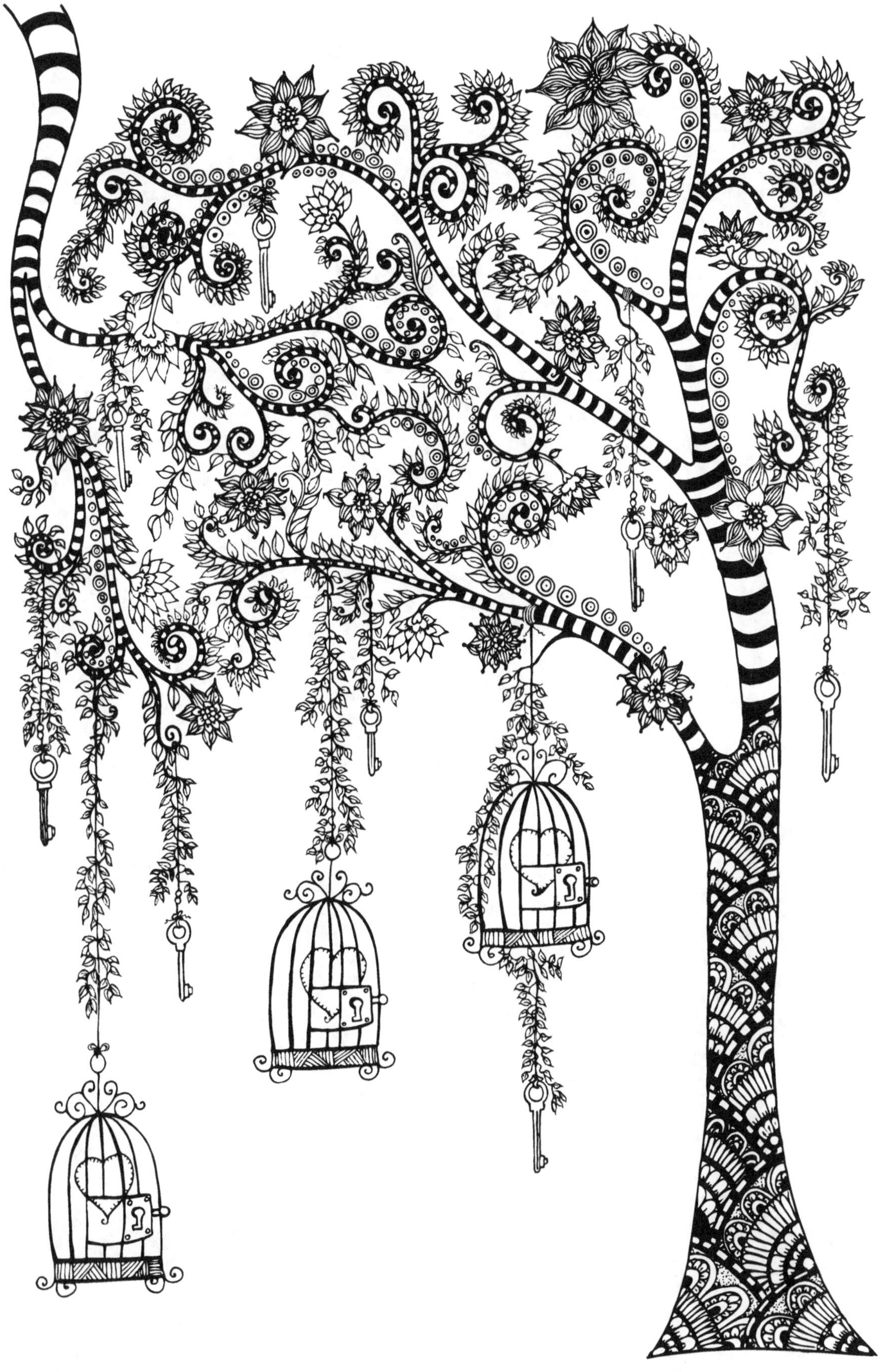

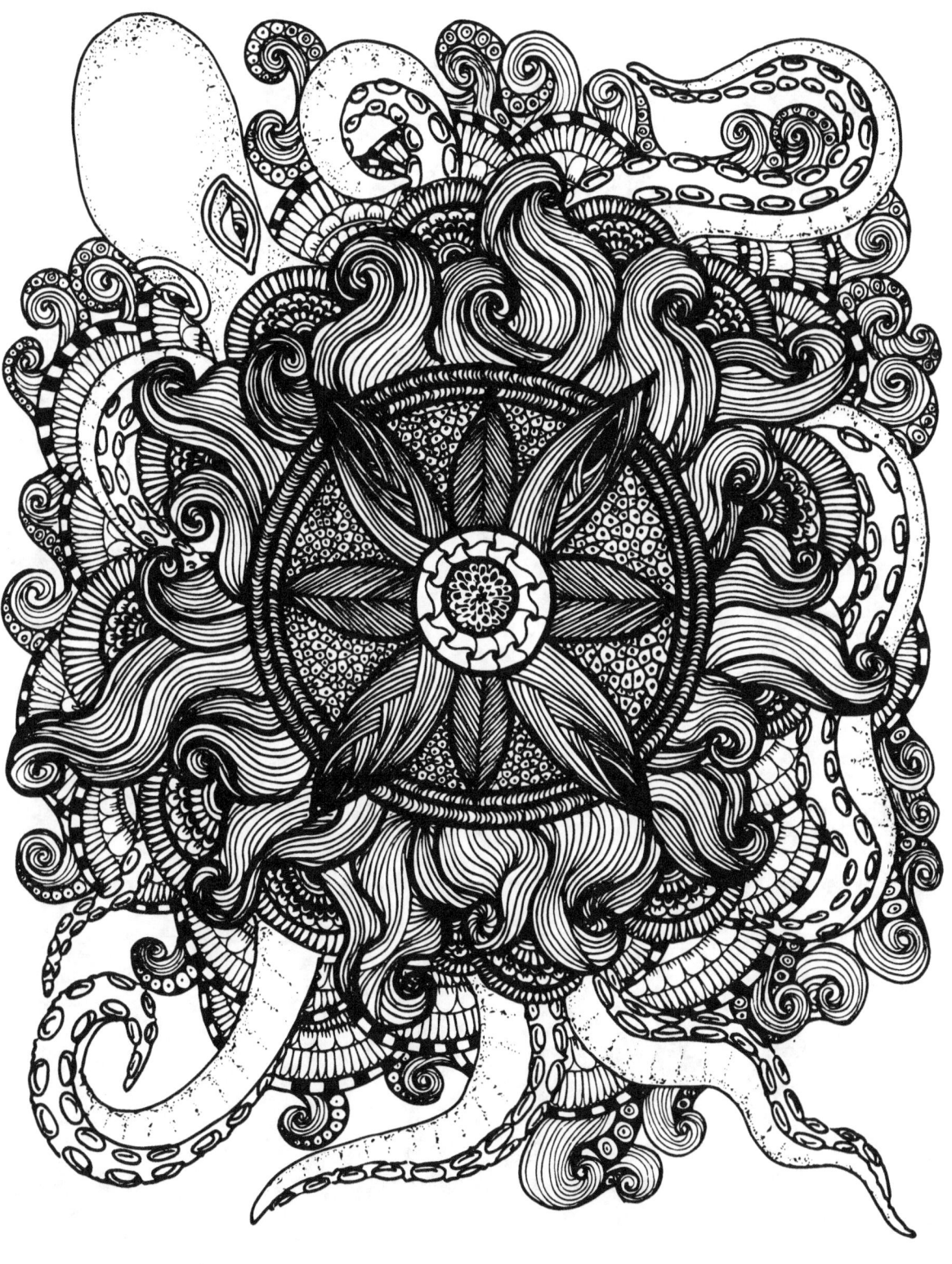

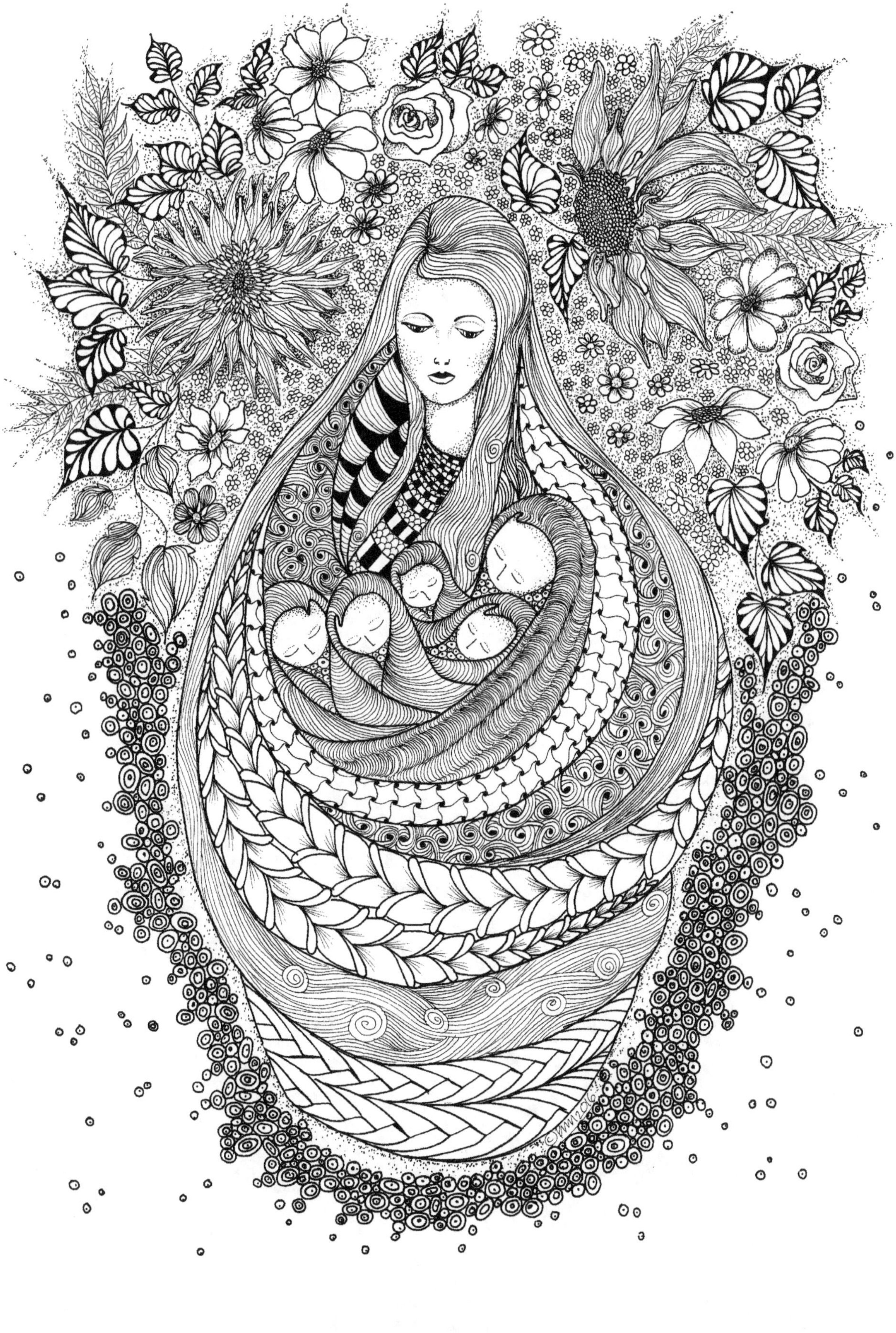

Artist:©IvetteRamosLevy Colorist:________

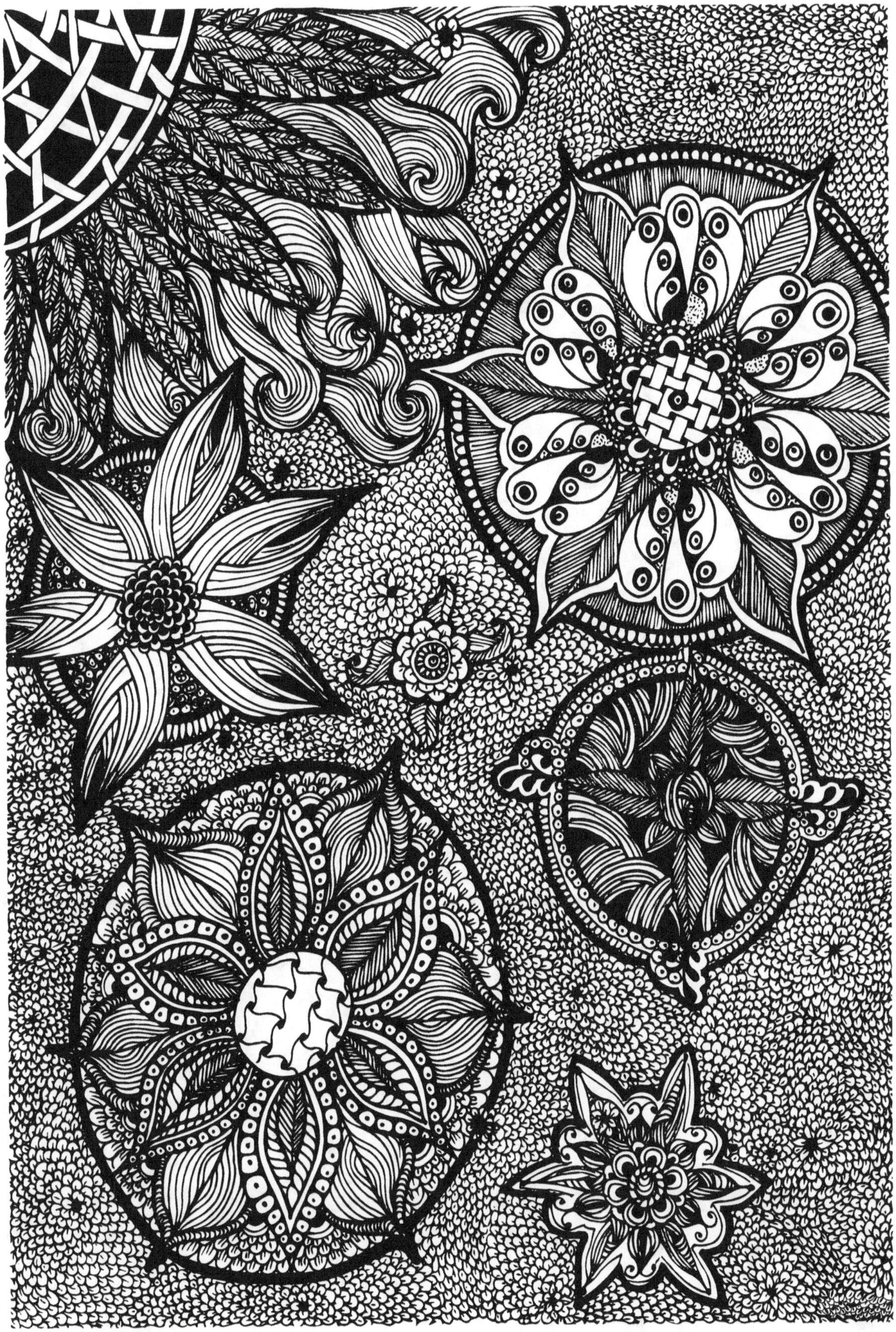

Artist:©IvetteRamosLevy Colorist:________

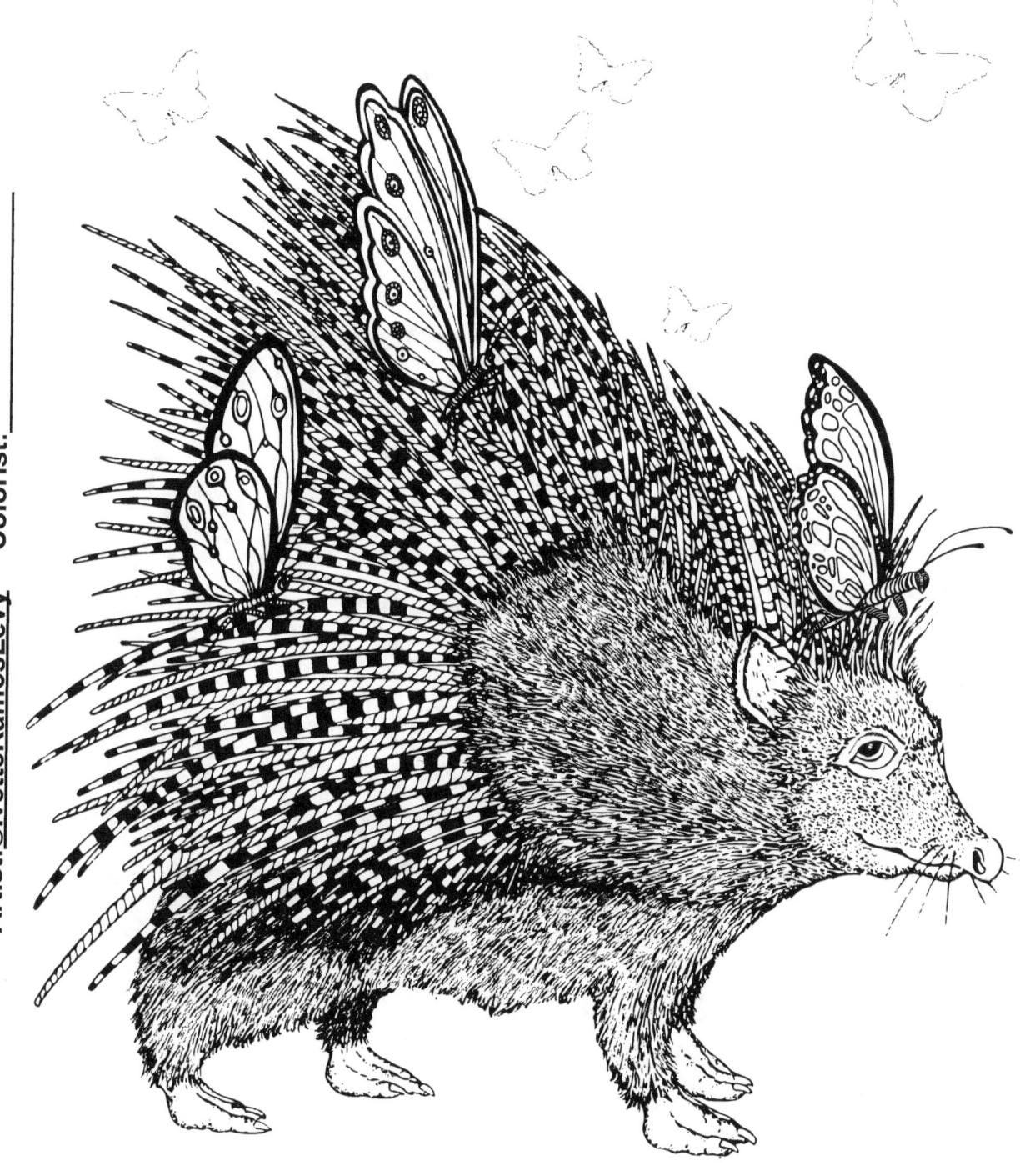

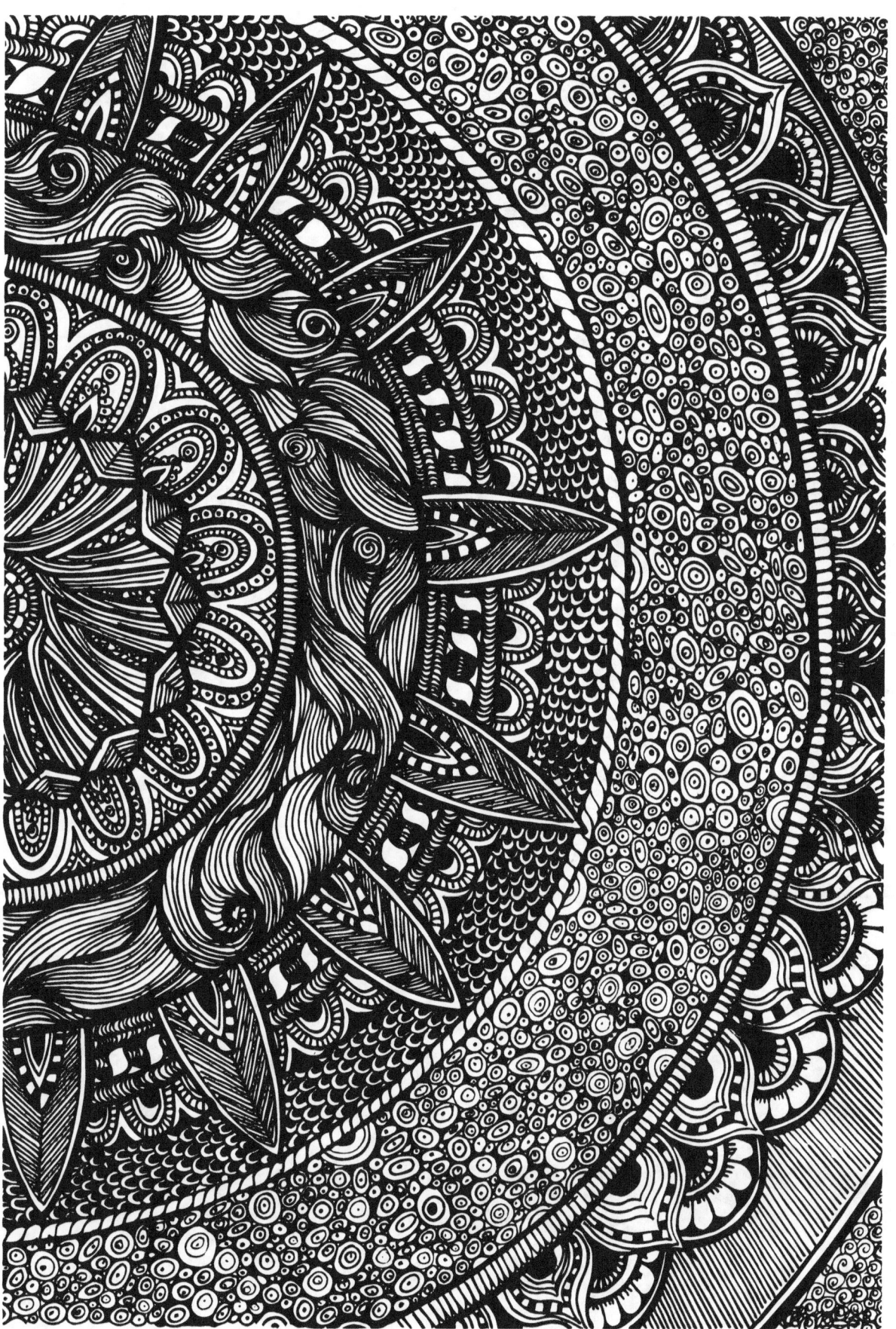

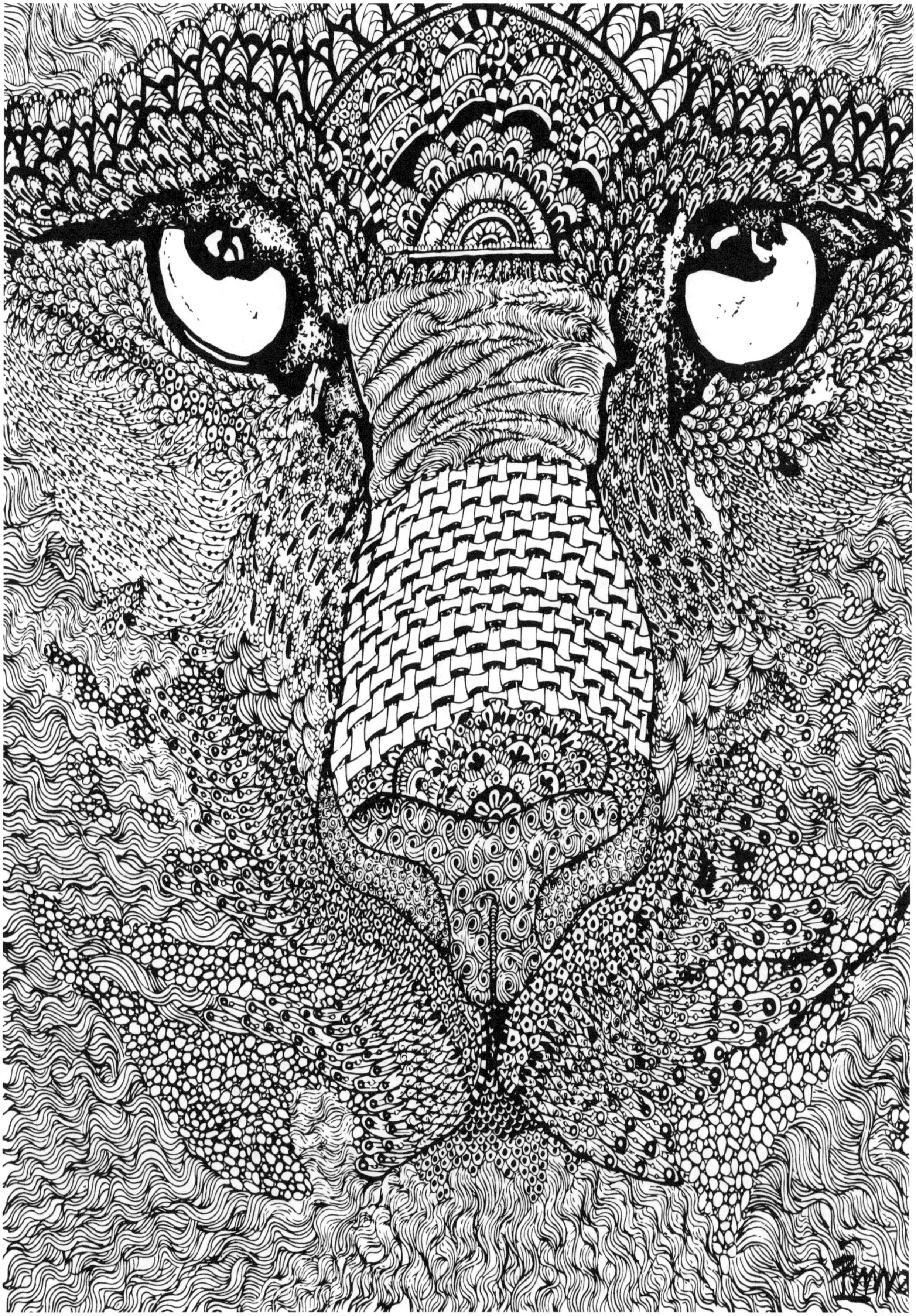

Artist:©IvetteRamosLevy Colorist:____________

Artist:©IvetteRamosLevy Colorist:__________

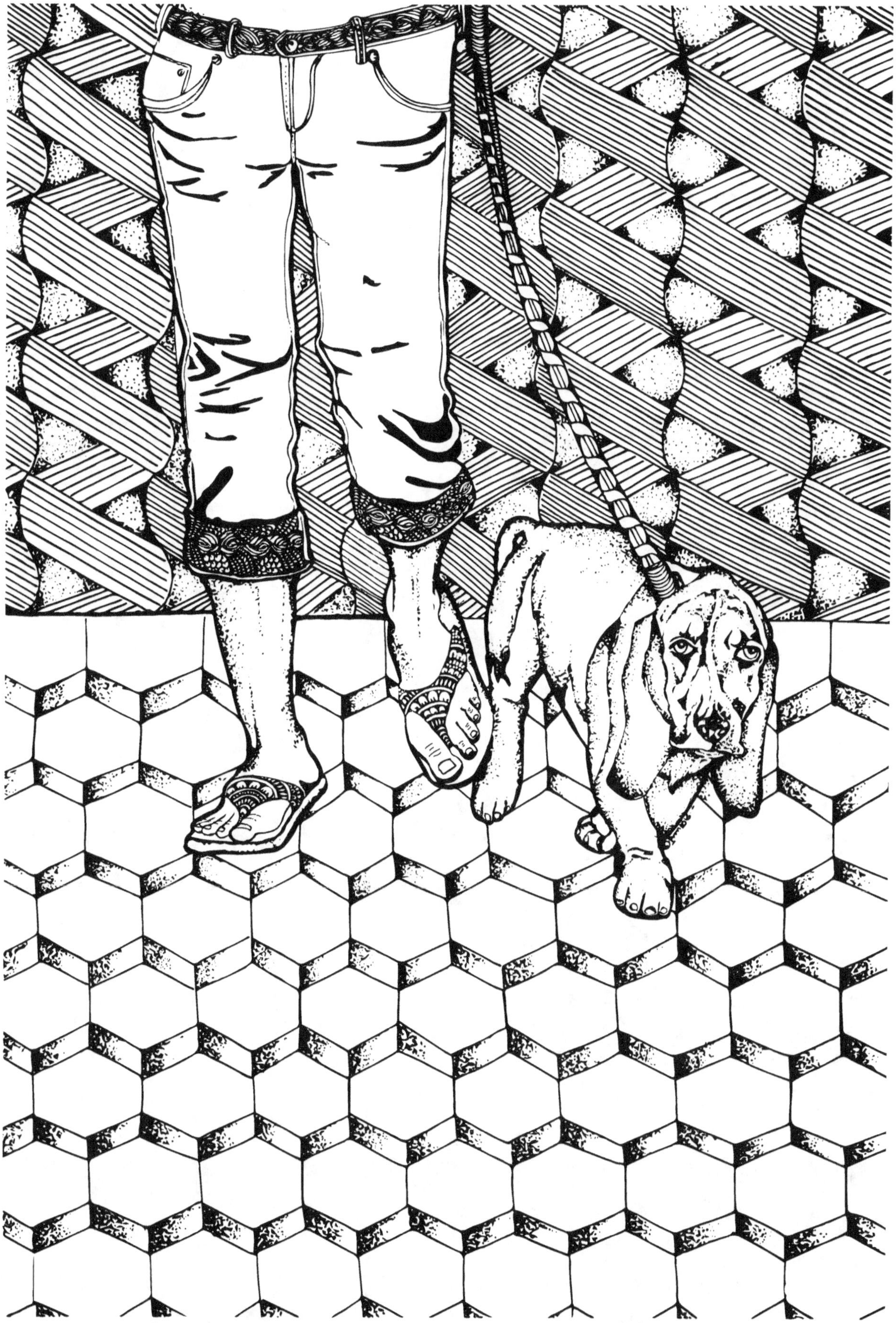

Colorist: _____

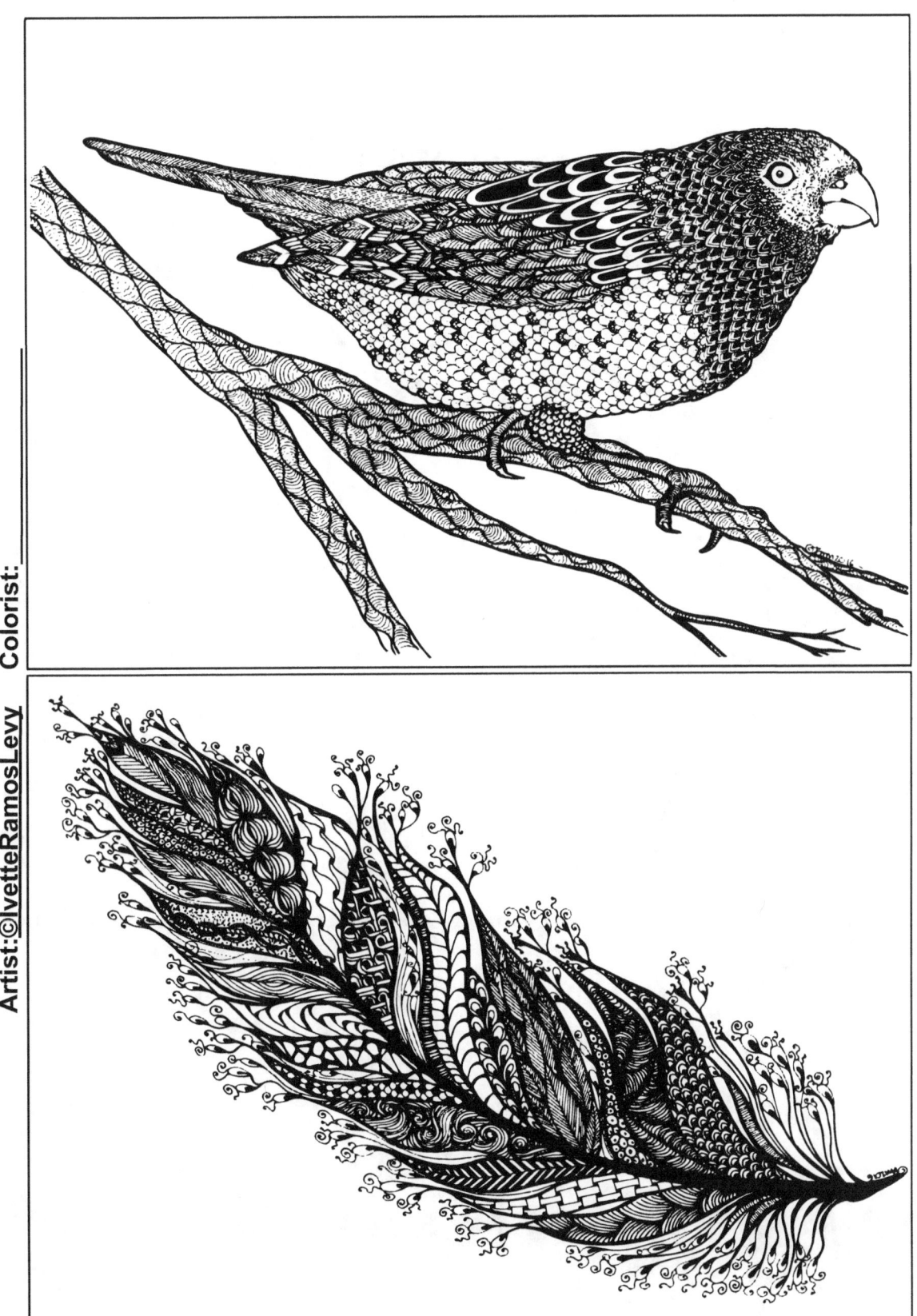

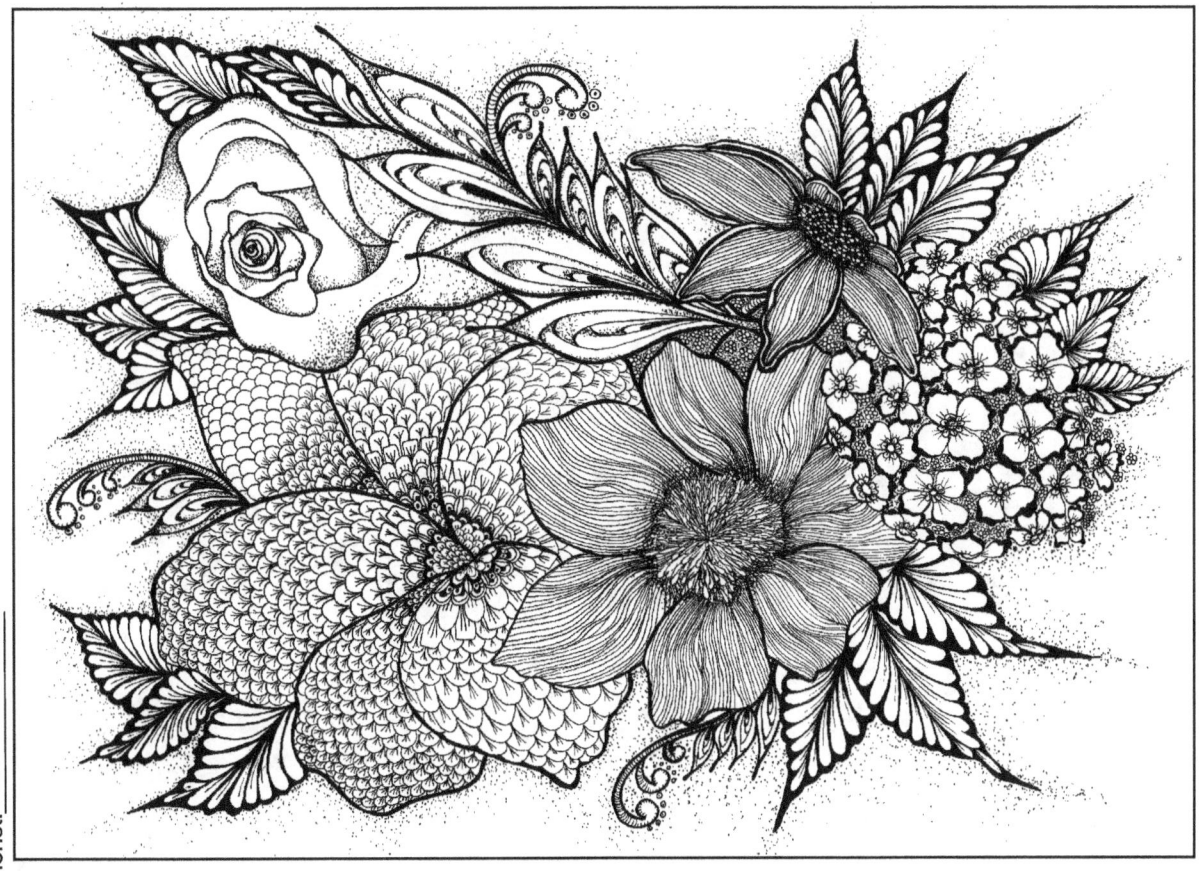

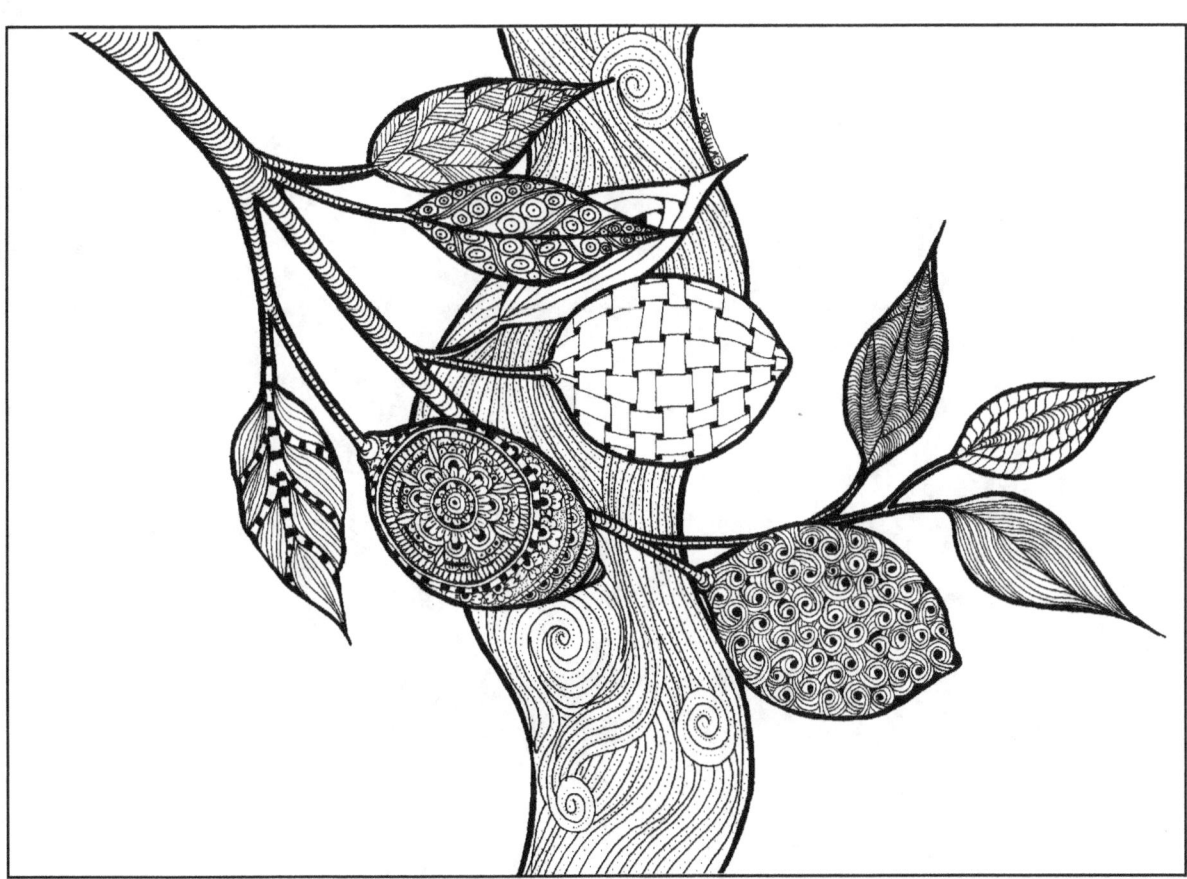

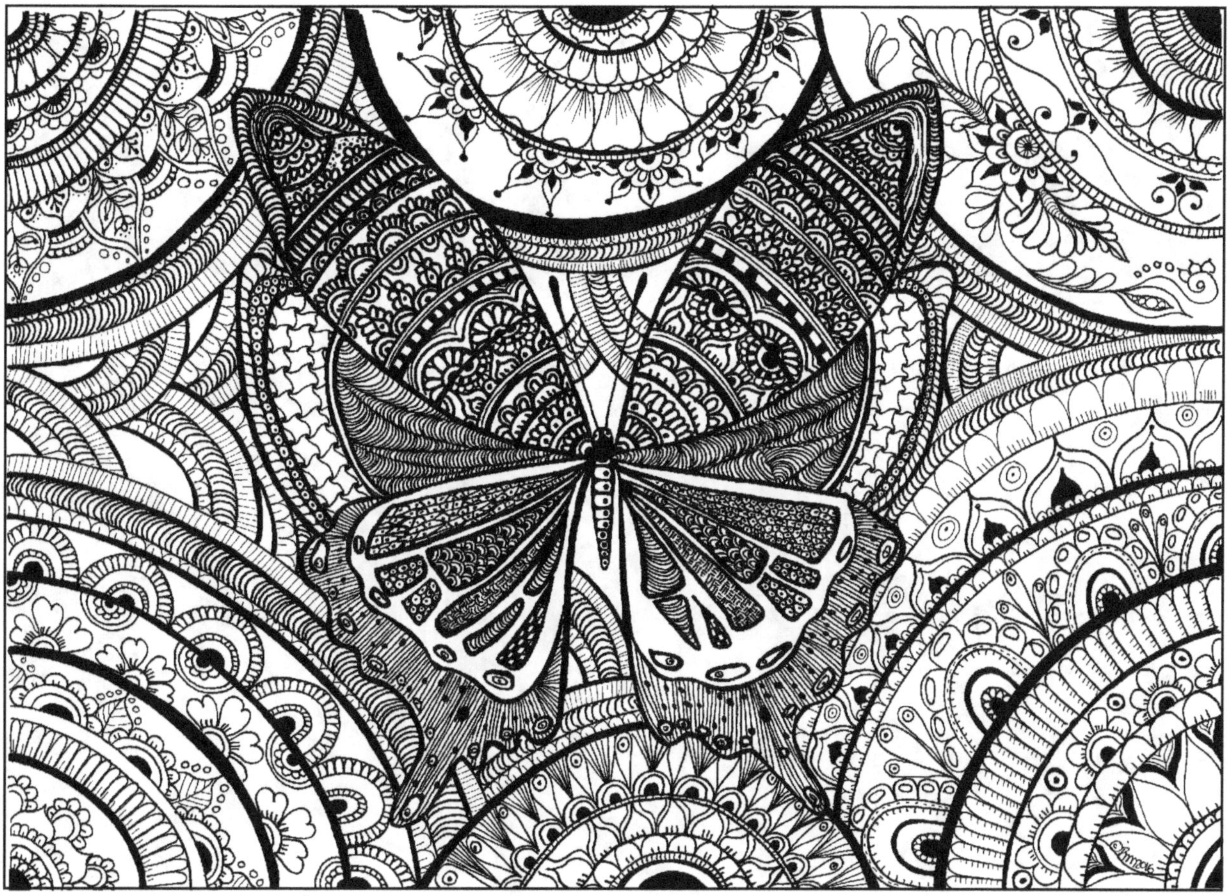

Artist:©IvetteRamosLevy

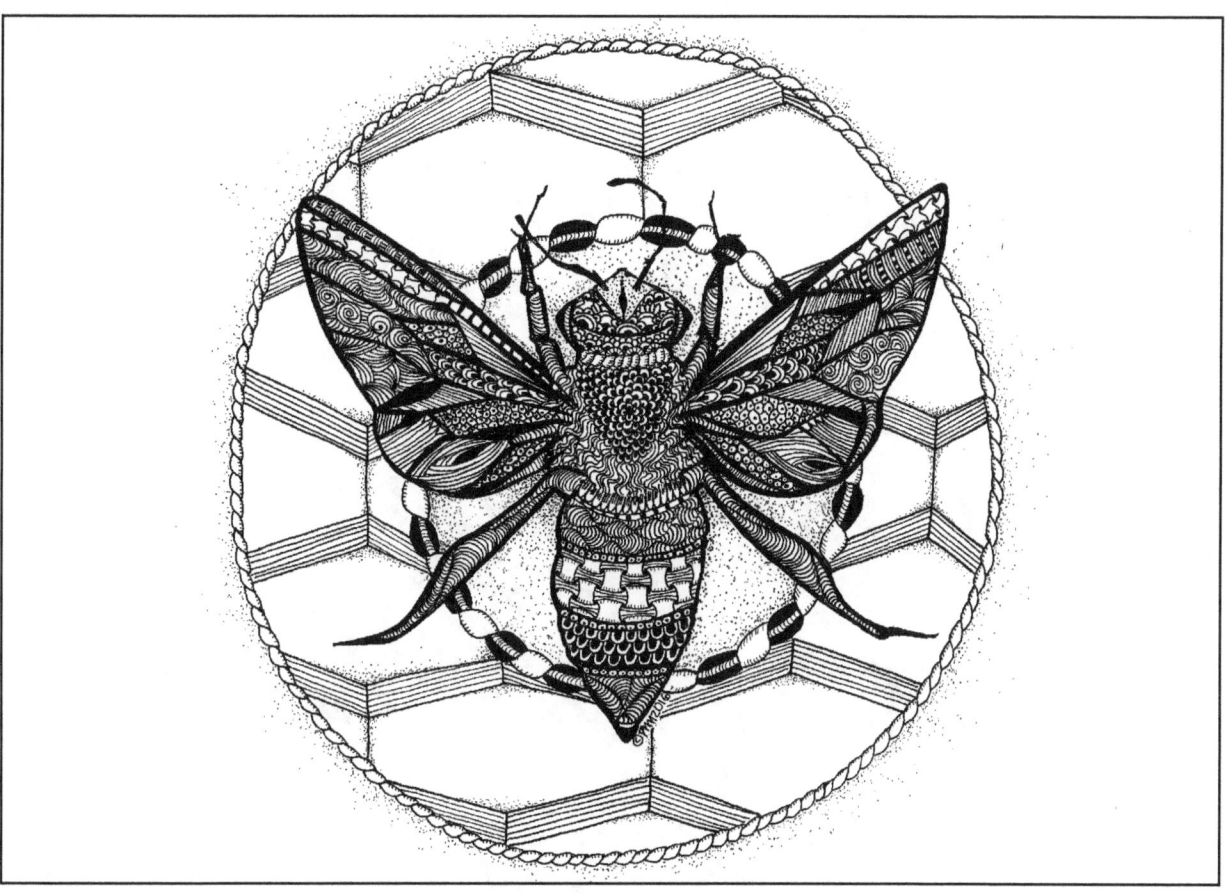

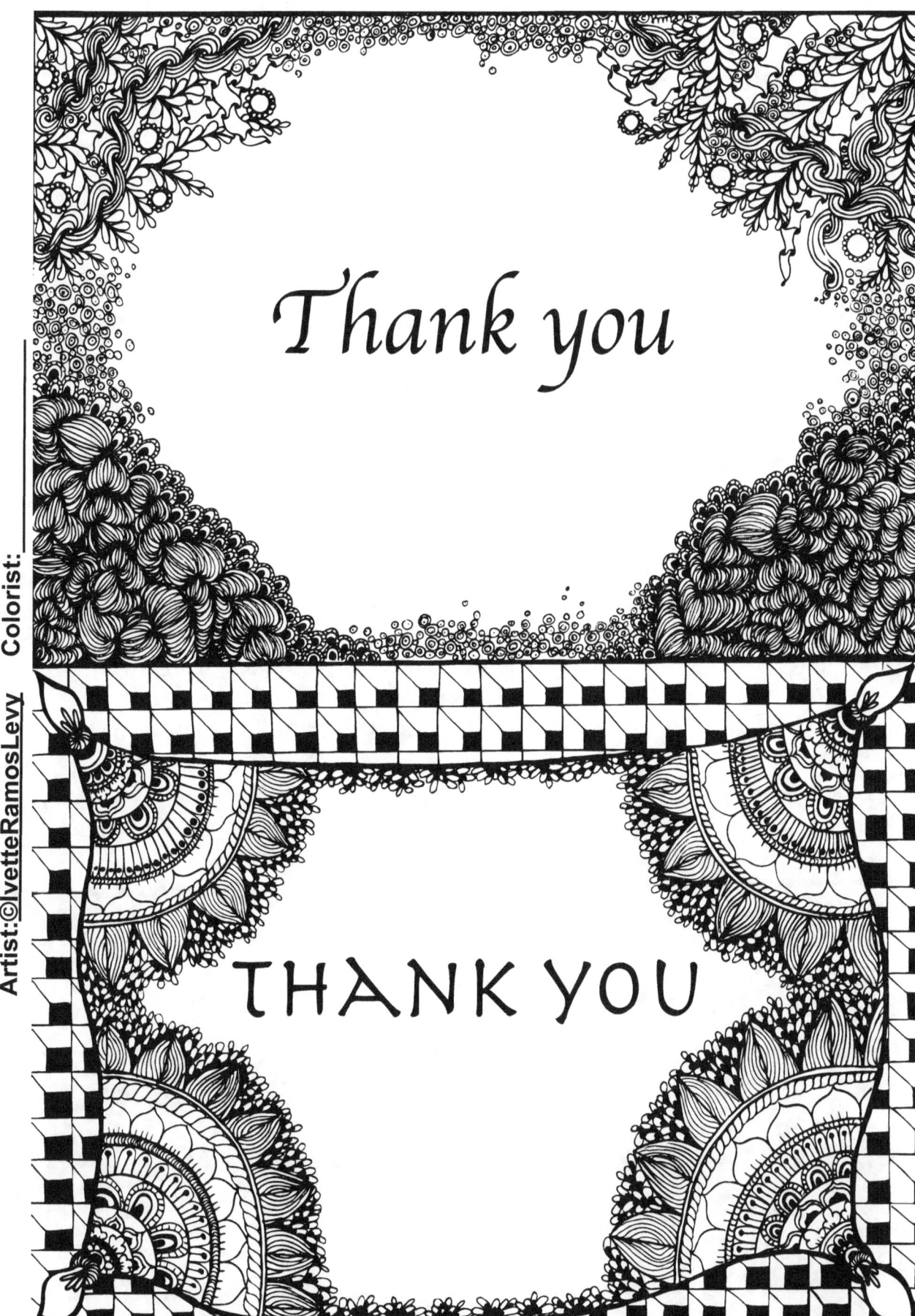

Thank you

THANK YOU

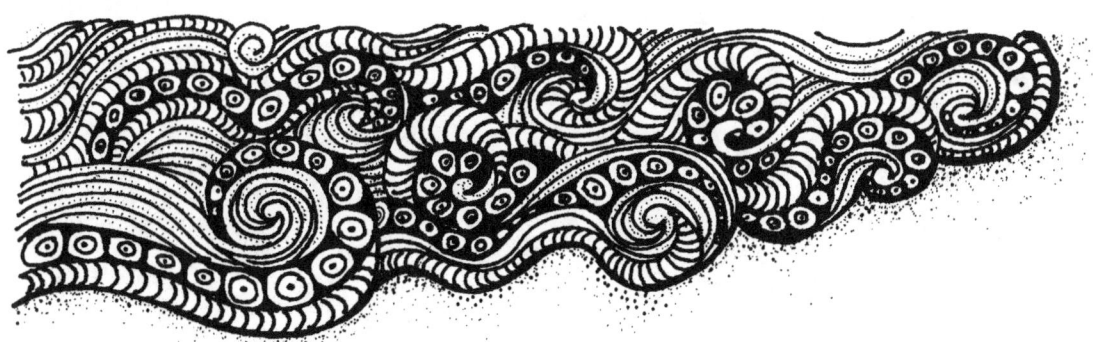

I hope you enjoyed coloring these illustrations
as much as I enjoyed creating them.
Thank you for purchasing my coloring book.
It gives me great joy to share my art with others.
Special thanks to God, my family, many close friends,
Coloring Book Author Support and
Authors of Coloring Books for Adults.
Please leave me a review and share your coloring
pages on my facebook page at:
ivette.ramoslevy

This journey has just begun!
To find my art work please visit:
www.ivetteramoslevy.com

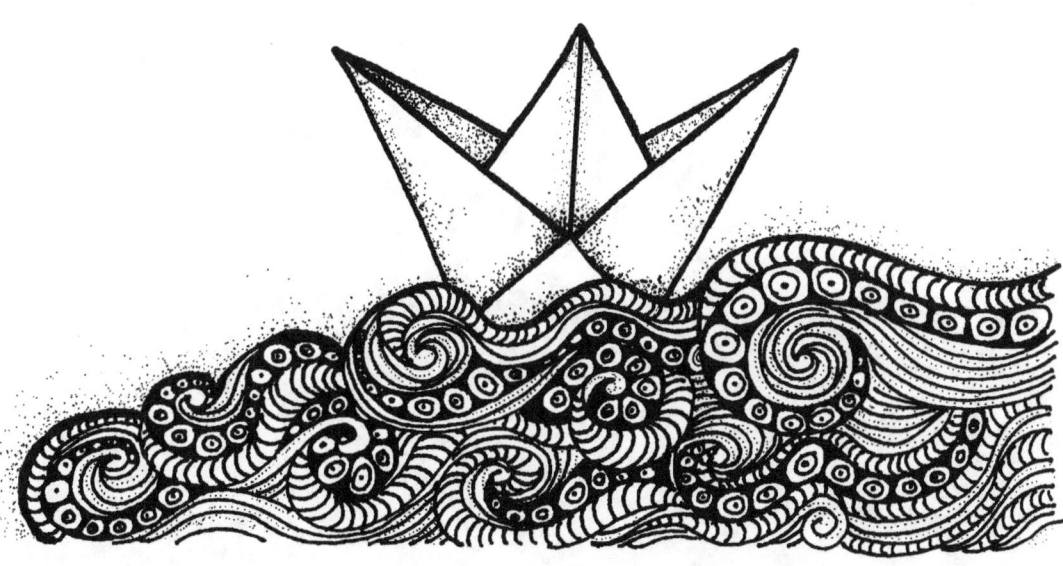

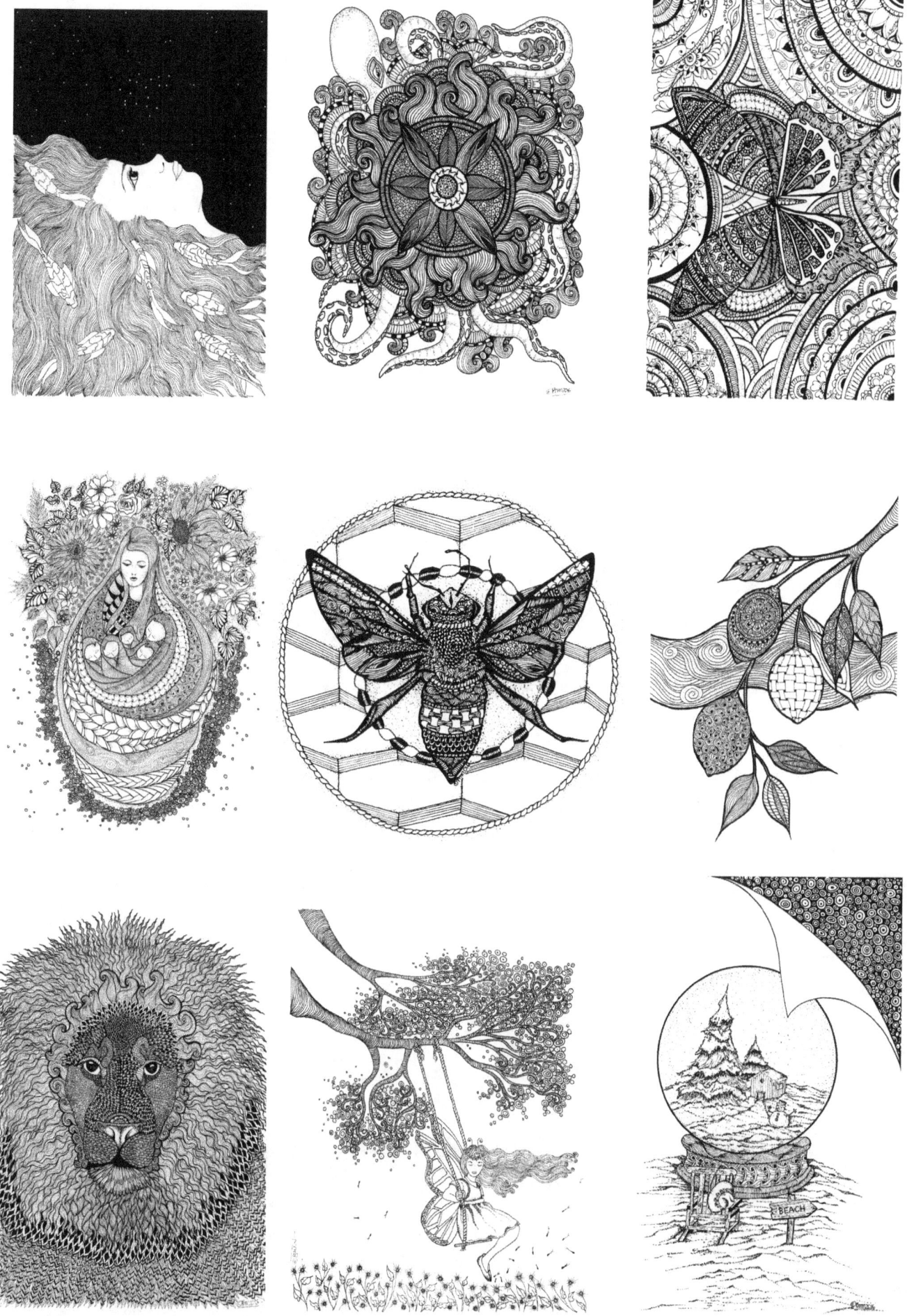